GUIDE TO THE

EAST MOJAVE
HERITAGE TRAIL

Fenner to Needles

Friends of the Mojave Road
RENDEZVOUS
1990

TED JENSEN

Needles

DESERT TORTOISE

The desert tortoise (*Xerobates agassizi*), which has the distinction of being the California State Reptile, is the largest reptile in the arid southwestern United States. It takes a tortoise 15 to 20 years to reach adult size. This long term inhabitant of the Mojave Desert was listed as a threatened species on April 2, 1990 by the U.S. Fish and Wildlife Service.

The threatened status has resulted from a rapid decrease in numbers in recent years that will affect long-term survival. While the factors behind this decrease are not completely understood in scientific terms, they may include habitat loss and segmenting; grazing by sheep and cattle; off-highway vehicles; vandalism, shooting, disease; excessive predation, especially by ravens; agricultural and residential development; and taking (kill, collection) of individuals form the wild. The taking of tortoises from the wild is prohibited by federal law as a result of their threatened status. The presence of an upper respiratory disease in wild tortoise populations increases the importance of not releasing pet tortoises back into the wild after being held in captivity. With all these problems facing the tortoise, it needs all the help it can get.

The Bureau of Land Management administers much of the important tortoise habitat throughout California, Arizona, and Nevada. Your cooperation in minimizing impact to tortoise populations is greatly appreciated and will aid in maintaining our fragile desert ecosystem.

TED JENSEN

GUIDE TO THE

EAST MOJAVE HERITAGE TRAIL

Fenner to Needles

by Dennis G. Casebier
and the
Friends of the Mojave Road

road log by
Neal Johns

maps by
R. N. "Bob" Martin

illustrated by
Ted Jensen

Tales of the Mojave Road
Publishing Company
HCR G, #15
Essex, California 92332
619-733-4482

Library of Congress Card Number
90-70195

ISBN 0-914224-19-0

Printed by
The A-to-Z Printing Company
of
Riverside, California

Binding by
National Bindery Company
of
Pomona, California

WARNING

TED JENSEN

WARNING

This *Guide to the East Mojave Heritage Trail* is **not** designed to serve as a survival manual. Desert travel always presents a risk of danger to life and property. Nobody can anticipate the full spectrum of difficulties that can be encountered by the desert traveler and absolutely no effort has been made to do that in this Guide. The next emergency that occurs on the desert will be something that is totally unanticipated by the participants, the *Friends of the Mojave Road,* the Bureau of Land Management, or anyone else. Therefore, those who choose to travel in the desert, whether it be on the **East Mojave Heritage Trail** making use of this Guide, or elsewhere, do so entirely at their own risk.

CONTENTS

MAPS

ON THE EAST MOJAVE HERITAGE TRAIL
USE CB CHANNEL 12

ACKNOWLEDGEMENTS

As with the Mojave Road, development of the EAST MOJAVE HERITAGE TRAIL (EMHT) has been a volunteer project. Many people have helped in numerous ways. All these efforts are greatly appreciated and vital to the project.

The *Friends of the Mojave Road* receive no resource support from any public agency. It is up to us to finance field trips, obtain research materials, procure photographic equipment and services, procure word processing equipment and services, and on and on. Many of you have donated equipment and your time and professional expertise in these areas. We thank you very much.

To publish each Guide has required that we raise more than $20,000 to cover the costs. The volunteers provide resources by paying for copies of the books in advance. We publicly thank all of you who have supported our project in this way.

Another major contribution is the time and effort spent by individuals and groups in the field doing exploration and scouting and testing the road logs and Guides prior to their being finalized. Great value is added to the Guides by this testing. We appreciate that effort very much.

Needless to say, we are always in need of money. Any project is stimulated and moves forward more gracefully if the machinery is lubricated with money.

Many of you have sent contributions and they have been extremely helpful. We refrain from listing you individually to protect your privacy.

We are greatly indebted to the "old-timers" and others who have granted interviews and permitted us to copy photographs. This helps us guarantee that the rich history of the East Mojave will be preserved. People we have interviewed on tape and whose photos we have copied in preparing material for the Guide to the Fourth Segment are the following: John Bentley, Milton Blair, Sr., Milton Blair, Jr., Joe Byers, J. D. McClanahan, Tom More, Betty (Pettit) Papierski, Doug & Pat Smith, Maurice & Lenna Swain. Thank you very much. If you have spent time in the East Mojave, or if you know of people who have, please send their names and addresses to the *Friends of the Mojave Road*, HCR G, #15, Essex, California 92332. It has been our universal experience that every "old-timer" has unique information to contribute.

Ted Jensen, Neal Johns, Bob & Marilyn Martin, and Jo Ann Smith have all contributed vitally to the overall success of the East Mojave Heritage Trail Project. Special graphics and tributes to them are included on the end sheets of this book.

Three of the Guides to the East Mojave Heritage Trail have sparkled with the beauty of wonderfully reproduced color photographs. This would not have been possible without the generosity and talents of Alan Siebert and Vojciech Maszekiewicz of MBM Graphics. Our heartfelt thanks for this work. The books would have been less than they are without this support.

Gene Compere, Gary Glover, Bill Kappele, Bill Lewis, and Herb Riggs have helped greatly with photographic processing. This is extremely important to our work in many respects. First, we need good photos (contemporary and historical) for the Guides. Second, and perhaps equally important, we need processing and printing of the large collection of historical photographs we are accumulating.

We owe a special thanks to A-to-Z Printing Company of Riverside, California. Eben, Jim, and Fran Dale, the principals of the company, have taken a personal interest in our publications and that has enriched our final products. Allison Taber, Millie Hinsvark, Leslie Schehl, and Bill Westwood have performed "above and beyond the call" and are deserving of our special thanks and praise.

While in the midst of preparing this Guide to the Fourth and Final Segment of the East Mojave Heritage Trail, I retired after 30 years in federal service as a scientist. We packed up my extensive collection of East Mojave historical materials, and moved bag and baggage to the Schoolhouse at Goffs. The logistics in making the move were horrendous, living quarters at Goffs were not adequate, and, in short, the obstacles were difficult. Still, we had to forge ahead and complete this book while continuing to produce Mojave Road Reports, pursue our oral history program, and make preparations for the RENDEZVOUS. But there wasn't time to fret. How many times did we say to ourselves: "When the going

11.

gets tough, that's when the tough get going!"

We made it, but not without the help of many *Friends of the Mojave Road.* I cannot list here everything that everyone did. But I am going to include a list of the names of those who helped. I expect I'll leave a few out and that of course is the natural consequence of trying to produce such a list. But to me it is worth the risk because I do so deeply appreciate all that you did and it came at such a critical time that I want you to know I will not forget. So here we go: Ed Alsip, Bill Bains, Bill & Nita Claypool, Fran Dale, Ron Demmit, Pat & Myr Deputy, Norma Dickey, Dan Fison, Dave Given, Gary Given, Rick Hughey, Paul Koehler, Bill Lewis, John Mathews, Dick MacPherson, Rick MacPherson, Richard Meyer, O. B. O'Brien, Tom Owens, Pete & Bonnie Panattoni, Steve Panattoni, Leroy & Linda Pilkenton, Hank Polonsky, Skip & Barbie Slavkin, Frank Sparks, Norm & Francie Takvam, Robert & Mary Jane Teitsworth, Frank Tomlinson, Jim & Bertha Wold, John Zupkofska.

This Guide is enriched through written contributions by a number of leading desert writers. Inputs are included from: Thomas Cooper, Ev Hayes, Mike McGill, Betty Papierski, Steven Pencall, Alan Romspert, Delmer G. Ross, and Jim Vernon.

Bill Bains, Dick MacPherson, and Rick MacPherson fabricated the Mail Box for the Fourth Segment, delivered it to the site with materials, and participated in its installation. They've done that for all four Segments of the East Mojave Heritage Trail for which they have our thanks.

The development of the East Mojave Heritage Trail has been pursued as a public service project in direct support of BLM. Without their approval and encouragement the project would not have proceeded. Ev Hayes, as Area Manager for BLM's Needles Resource Area encouraged us to enter into the project and assisted us through the first three segments. Then, in this book, he continued that support, although now working with BLM in Nevada, by providing an article on Camp Clipper that is produced in the appendix. Ev's successor in the Needles office, Rich Fagan, provided continuity in direct BLM support on the ground. Our thanks to Rich and the many members of his staff who have helped in various way, and especially to Phil Damon who has served as our point of contact for the EMHT project for the last two segments.

Support for our project has come from the district and state levels. We would not have had a project without the approval and support of Jerry Hillier, Director of BLM's California Desert District, and Ed Hastey, Director for BLM in all of California. Many thanks to these busy executives who have found the time to lend a hand in our direction when it has been needed.

Our thanks to Congressman Jerry Lewis, representative for Calfiornia's 35th District, which includes the East Mojave and the entire area embraced by the East Mojave Heritage Trail, for his support to our project and for providing leadership to keep the desert free at the federal level.

Dennis G. Casebier
September 23, 1990

AUTOGRAPHS

EAST MOJAVE HERITAGE TRAIL

Development of the EAST MOJAVE HERITAGE TRAIL as an interpreted backcountry four-wheel drive trail is an extension of the Mojave Road project. With the Mojave Road, we had a 130-mile segment of an old transdesert wagon road that was in very much the same condition as it was in the 1880s when it fell out of use as a route to cross the desert.

Before proceeding to develop the Mojave Road as a recreation trail, the question of what kind of trail it should be was examined carefully. In 1975 I hiked the entire trail myself, taking eight days to make the trip. My thought at that point was perhaps it should be made into a hiking trail.

It was a wonderful experience, but one from which I emerged believing that that wasn't the way to do it. That belief has been borne out by subsequent experiences. Even with all the publicity the trail has received, and the attractions that exist along it for hiking, probably not a dozen people have hiked the trail in the 15 years that have passed since I did it in 1975. Cross-country hiking in the desert is not popular and may never be.

Many people climb mountains in the desert. They use one of the many access roads to approach the edge of the mountain mass and then hike up into the mountain area. Distance hiking across the broad valleys between the separated mountain ranges is another matter. It is much more enjoyable to pass through these areas slowly in a vehicle. At first, I was unwilling to lead vehicles over the trail. I was afraid it would damage it somehow.

I should have known better. After all, these are established roads. If vehicles drive on them, they'll look more like roads, more like they looked in the old days. Also, a certain amount of use will prevent roads from disappearing altogether, as was happening in a few places with the Mojave Road.

In 1980 I was approached by a member-club of the Associated Blazers of California. They wanted me to show them over the Mojave Road; I cautiously consented. I rode in one of their vehicles. They were all equipped with CB radios. Beginning at the Colorado River, and continuing on for two days, 100 miles west to Soda Lake, I lectured on history, flora, fauna, management, and other subjects, almost continously.

It was like magic. A classroom on wheels! No damage was done to the desert. No one was testing their machine. They were there to experience the wonders of the desert and to learn about it. I was thrilled by the experience and determined to try it again.

I did try it again for there was no shortage of off-highway vehicle groups interested in this kind of experience. That's how development of the Mojave Road Recreation Trail got started. Soon the *Friends of the Mojave Road* was formed. We entered into a voluntary agreement with BLM to develop the trail. Development consisted of marking it out with small piles of rocks called cairns and preparing and publishing a written guide.

The GUIDE TO THE MOJAVE ROAD was styled to provide the same experience for anyone with the book that we had provided to others by lecturing over CB. The entire text is laid out by miles west from the Colorado River. Almost everything you might want to say to someone passing through the East Mojave is prompted by something you see along the way. That formed the basis for the structure of the Guide. If you go out there today

16.

and see a caravan of vehicles inching along over the trail, likely you'll find someone has the Guide open, following it and learning as the group goes along.

Several years of this experience show us that this use, to date, has done no harm to the environment. A trip over the Mojave Road is rich in educational, spiritual, and recreational values. The participant is preoccupied with the wonders of the desert and the learning experience. No damage occurs. Drivers on the trail have a mind-set to move on. They pass slowly through the desert and keep on moving to the end.

The *Friends of the Mojave Road* firmly believe this backcountry use of the desert can be pursued in the California Desert as well as the East Mojave National Scenic Area at this time without doing damage. It is the right kind of experience for those who yearn for freedom and want to enjoy the great natural beauty and cultural charm of the East Mojave.

At the conclusion of the Mojave Road project, we were encouraged by many people to develop other trails. The abandoned berm of the old Tonopah and Tidewater Railroad was recommended by some, as were other routes. We examined the possibilities carefully and ultimately settled on the approach of a 660-mile closed loop through the desert that would make use of all sorts of existing roads and trails. For awhile the traveler will be on an old mining road, then he might visit a mining district, then he might be on a power line or a gas line road, then an old wagon road, an abandoned railroad berm, or a water line road on a cattle ranch.

The 660-mile loop has been laid out carefully and a guide developed like the Guide for the Mojave Road. A resource of inestimable value is being created for people who enjoy the backcountry -- people who are looking for a positive, educational experience. Two years were spent exploring the desert to identify an appropriate preliminary route and to develop rough road logs. We had hoped in the beginning to obtain financial support for this from Government or industry. That did not develop. The potential is there, but it is too hard and there are too many strings attached.

To go forward with the entire 660-mile trail at once was not practical with no substantive support outside our own resources. We therefore determined to develop one segment at a time. For the initial segment, we selected the 171.6 miles of the EAST MOJAVE HERITAGE TRAIL between Needles and old Ivanpah on the northeast side of Clark Mountain. The Guide to that portion was published October 10, 1987. The Guide to the Second Segment, Ivanpah to Rocky Ridge, was published October 8, 1988. It extended the trail from Mile 171.6 through Mile 350.3. The Guide to the Third Segment, Rocky Ridge to Fenner was published October 7, 1989. It extended the trail from Mile 350.3 through Mile 508.3. The present book is the Guide to the Fourth Segment, Fenner to Needles, and the mileage is extended to 660.0.

One motivation for defining the EAST MOJAVE HERITAGE TRAIL is the increasing and heavy use the Mojave Road is receiving. In the year ending 1988, more than 2,000 people signed in at the Mojave Road Mail Box provided for that purpose along the trail. As reflected by the lack of damage to the trail and the country through which it passes, this is not yet too much traffic. But the demand continues to increase. The EAST MOJAVE HERITAGE TRAIL, now completed, provides the equivalent of more than four trails the length of the

Mojave Road.

There is much concern about preservation of essential values in the Mojave Desert today, and rightfully so. One of the values that ranks high with the people using it is freedom. We are at a time when we will lose our freedom to use the desert if we don't take very good care of it.

Tread lightly as you go over the EAST MOJAVE HERITAGE TRAIL. Recognize that you are passing through a living museum. All around you are exhibits that are unlabeled and unprotected. Take great care not to damage any of them. This book is a partial Guide to these resources. It is designed to help you understand the desert itself and the lives and activities of people who have passed through before you, as well as those who still earn their livelihood there.

Friends of the Mojave Road
assemble at Fenner at Mile 508.3 on the
EAST MOJAVE HERITAGE TRAIL
preparing for a trip over the Fourth Segment.

25 November 1989
Dennis Casebier Photo

GENERAL GUIDELINES

There are no signs telling you where to go on the 151.7 miles of the EAST MOJAVE HERITAGE TRAIL between Fenner and Needles. You must rely on the maps and the descriptive narrative in this book, and rock cairns placed along the way. Elevations are given at almost every entry.

When you travel the trail from Fenner toward Needles, the cairns will be on your right side. There is considerable variation in the size of the cairns as the rocks have a tendency to tumble. This might be caused by people, cattle, wind, earth tremors, faulty construction, or a combination of things. When you see that this has happened, you may want to stack the rocks back up or do whatever rebuilding seems to be required to help the next traveler.

On the Mojave Road Recreation Trail, an effort was made to put cairns at every intersection with other roads (however faint the roads), at major washes where the road might be difficult to follow after floods, and at other places as it was deemed necessary or convenient. There was no effort to put cairns at regular intervals, but where the way was confusing we put them close together. Frequently in these instances one cairn was placed in sight of the next one. On the EAST MOJAVE HERITAGE TRAIL, on the other hand, there was no formal program to put up cairns. In most instances, the cairns are being erected by travelers using the Trail. Generally these cairns are erected in accordance with the practice used for the Mojave Road. Be prepared, however, for long stretches with no cairns.

You are not left with cairns alone to guide you

over the Trail. More important are the specially drawn maps. The small-scale map (page 33) covers a large area of the East Mojave and is the key to the large-scale maps. Generally speaking, the small-scale map is used to locate the EAST MOJAVE HERITAGE TRAIL from modern roads while the large-scale maps are used to follow the Trail after you get on it.

The most important feature in the log is the mileage numbers. There are two sets of numbers. The series on the left side of the page are the miles from Needles and start with Mile 508.3 at Fenner and run continously to Mile 660.0 at Needles. The mileages at the end of each entry give you the distance to the next described feature.

There are no mileage indicators on the ground or along the Trail: they appear only in the Guide, on the maps, and in the log. Refer to these mileages for the narrative directions necessary to enable you to follow the Trail. History, flora, fauna, and other subjects of interest are also keyed for these mileages. Directions for staying on the Trail are given in **bold face type,** whereas other information presented in the main part of the book is given in ordinary type. This Guide differs from the earlier volumes in this series in that extensive subjects are referenced in the main body of the book, but they have been reproduced in an appendix of special topics.

To drive the Trail, watch the maps as you go along, read the narrative that goes with the country you're passing through, and all the while watch for any cairns that serve as a check that you're on the right track. To highlight that part of the text that provides directions for staying on the Trail, a single asterisk (*) has been placed at the beginning of such information. To provide additional emphasis for particularly <u>significant</u> directions, two asterisks (* *) are used.

The mileages along the Trail are as accurate as we could measure them. You cannot expect your own odometer readings to agree exactly. It will be helpful to you to check the accuracy of your odometer against the small mile markers on the Interstate routes as you drive out to the desert. This will enable you to establish a constant factor with which to reconcile the mileages you observe on your odometer with those in the Guide. The mileages are useful to tell you where you are within normal odomoter accuracy. If you are a member of the Automobile Club of Southern California, their San Bernardino County Map for this area is excellent, but does not cover all of the roads we use.

VEHICLE AND OTHER REQUIREMENTS
MISCELLANEOUS WARNINGS

Most of the country traversed by the HERITAGE TRAIL is desert wilderness, although it is not officially designated as "Wilderness" in the technical sense. (The HERITAGE TRAIL does pass through several Wilderness Study Areas -- these are indicated on the maps.) In many places, the HERITAGE TRAIL is far removed from civilization -- days may pass without your seeing anyone. The distances to services on the Fourth Segment can be great. It is a place of remarkable beauty and solitude. Yet it can be a place of great danger if something goes wrong and the traveler finds himself short on equipment or knowledge of what to do. THIS GUIDE IS NOT A SURVIVAL BOOK. If you are inexperienced in desert travel or if your knowledge of what equipment you should have or what to do in emergencies is lacking, don't expect this book to correct these deficiencies. You must get your knowledge of desert survival elsewhere.

If you are traveling the EAST MOJAVE HERITAGE TRAIL, the following suggestions should be considered in your plans and equipment selections:

***There must be more than one vehicle in the group.

***All vehicles must have four-wheel drive.

***Have sufficient gasoline to travel the entire Fourth Segment without replenishment. Unlike the other segments of the EMHT, there are no intermediate points for refueling. For many this will mean you must carry extra cans of gasoline or leave the Trail to obtain gasoline at Vidal Junction or Havasu Lake.

***Carry sufficient emergency food and water to last a week.

***Know what you are going to do in case of snake bite or other serious injury.

***File a travel plan with officials or friends.

***As you travel the Trail, develop the policy that each vehicle is responsible for keeping the vehicle behind in sight. If necessary, wait at each turn or crossroad for the vehicle behind to appear.

***All vehicles should have shovels, snatch ropes, jack,

tow chains, or similar devices. It is advisable to have at least one vehicle with a winch.

***After a rain, leave considerable space between vehicles. Then, if you should hit a soft area, only one vehicle will get stuck and the others can pull it out.

***Many off-highway drivers let some of the air out of their tires for better flotation in sand. Check with your tire expert before doing this for proper procedure with your tires.

***If you plan to go from Fenner all the way to Needles, you'll need at least two full days: a minimum of three days is recommended.

***It can be extremely hot in the low country in summer and much of the Fourth Segment is in this lower country. Many travelers will find this segment to be unacceptably hot during the summer months. At the same time, you must be prepared for very cold nights in winter months. Weather-wise, the best months to travel the HERITAGE TRAIL are October and November and March and April.

***The firmness of sand varies significantly depending upon how moist it is. If it has rained within a month or two of when you pass through a sandy area, and if the weather has not been hot and winds have not been strong, the sand may be firm. Later in the year, after it has been hot and much time has passed without rain, the road that was so easy and firm before, may now be a trap of soft powdery sand. Watch for it. Proceed cautiously into areas where sand has drifted. Leave considerable space between vehicles so only one gets stuck if you hit unexpectedly bad sand.

***"Never camp in washes or stream beds in desert country" is a wise rule to follow. Flash floods of unbelievable intensity can appear without warning. In the area covered by this segment of the HERITAGE TRAIL, the worst storms of the type that give rise to flash flooding occur in August and September. Winter storms occur also, but they tend to be of much less intensity.

***The county roads are one of the most dangerous features of traveling in the East Mojave. There are a number of fairly well maintained county roads that serve the region. It is very easy to go too fast on these roads. Somehow they trick you into going too fast, then first thing you know you're heading into a curve that is poorly banked and is sharper than it looked. You "lose it" and skid around the corner. The lucky ones grip the wheel more tightly and slow down as they regain their composure beyond the curve. The unlucky ones roll over or run off the road. Many very serious single car accidents have occurred this way on the gravel and dirt roads of the East Mojave. Even the blacktop roads can be dangerous. There is a temptation to drive at freeway speeds, but the roads are not properly constructed for that. Also, this is open-range cattle country.

***Drive in four-wheel drive when on dirt roads. It'll cost you a little in gas mileage, but it gives you better control and the tires will slip less and consequently do less damage to the road surface for the benefit of the environment.

***Require that all vehicles in your caravan have CB radios. It will add much to your outing to be able to communicate while underway. Most people use Channel 12 on the EAST MOJAVE HERITAGE TRAIL.

DESERT ETIQUETTE

A tour of the HERITAGE TRAIL should be a positive and socially uplifting experience. The traveler needs to open his mind to the desert, to the narrative in this Guide, and to the reality of the desert around him. If he does, he'll emerge from traveling over the Trail better informed about the natural and human history of the desert and with a frame of mind more optimistic and positive.

This off-highway vehicle experience is not a contest or challenge with the land or with other travelers. The challenge to the vehicle user is to experience the natural and cultural wonders of a harsh desert region. Satisfy yourself that your style of use will not result in damage to the environment, to your vehicle, or to yourself. Indeed, part of the challenge today is for us to enjoy the freedom of a tour like this through the East Mojave without doing any damage at all. If we are not able to do that, then it is clear our privileges will be curtailed. We will lose our freedom. Be conscious of that at all times. Treat the desert gently at all times. It is extremely vulnerable.

The freedom with which we are permitted to travel through this desert country, together with its great natural beauty, including scenery, flora, and fauna, are the essential and fundamental values of this experience. These values are perishable. Never has the admonishment "abuse it and you'll lose it" had more direct application. It is a fact that this public land belongs to you and me, but we do not have the right to use it in any way that damages its essential values.

Nobody will be looking over your shoulder. You are free to behave however you wish. We believe the following basic ideas of behavior should be followed to guarantee that we will all continue to be free to pursue this experience, and to preserve and protect the vital elements of the desert's perishable resources.

Put yourself for a moment in the position of the cattle ranchers. Be respectful of them and their property. Be friendly to them, and they will be friendly back. Be understanding if they act a little suspicious. They have reason to be concerned. Their livelihood is out there wandering around virtually unprotected. We mention the cattle industry specifically because the Trail passes through so much cattle country and because their property is so exposed. Some of the roads we use were built by ranchers and are maintained by them. The same advice applies to other desert users you might meet. Do not spend more than 30 minutes in the vicinity of places where cattle water because the half-wild cattle will be afraid to come in. It is important that they have water every day. Do not camp within 600 feet of such a watering place. If you encounter loose cattle in the road, drive slowly to avoid causing them to run, especially in the heat. When you pass through gates in the range fences, leave them open or closed as you find them.

Stay on the road, except to park or camp. Scenic quality is an essential part of this experience. Random vehicle tracks will spoil it. You are permitted to camp within 300 feet of established trails, unless otherwise directed. In the East Mojave National Scenic Area, your camp must be within 20 feet of established roads (i.e., alongside the disturbed area) and in areas previously used for camping

Take all your trash home. If the other fellow has been more careless, help us all out. Take his trash home too. Remember, if you haul it in, haul it out!

Bring your own firewood. The desert does not offer enough. Gathering dead and down wood for "casual" use is allowed at the present time (free use -- no permit required) for use in the desert, but cutting of live wood is not permitted anywhere. "Casual" use means enough for one fire for one night.

Bring all the guns you want, but please don't discharge them during your HERITAGE TRAIL experience. The noise has a negative impact on the outing. Don't kill anything unnecessarily, even a Mojave green rattlesnake. This is not a killing experience. "Live and let live" as you pass over the HERITAGE TRAIL. Go shoot somewhere else, some other time.

Most damage to historical and archeological sites on the desert comes in tiny increments. Ordinary people, with no malice of forethought, sometimes do little things they think won't matter. Say, they take a stone from a wall for a souvenir. In time it loses its identity and becomes just another rock. Back on the desert it was a vital part of a historical structure that people enjoyed seeing. Others come along and do the same thing. The accumulated effect is major. With the increasing number of visitors, a historical structure can be ruined in a short time. Please leave everything for the next fellow to enjoy, just as you did. Take home your pictures; take home your memories; and take home the feeling that, as far as you are concerned, everything will be the same when you go back.

In a few places, the HERITAGE TRAIL passes through areas where there is unmarked private land. This Guide does not provide data to tell you when you are in the vicinity of private land. BLM publishes land status maps that can be used for this. There could be nervousness about increased traffic on the HERITAGE TRAIL by landowners adjacent to it. Our objective is to allay their concerns through our good citizenship. Of course, each of us is personally responsible to behave lawfully and with courtesy and respect for private property of all kinds that might be encountered on the desert.

Be extremely careful of the wildlife on the desert. It is a harsh land and some of the denizens of the desert have a harsh and even threatening appearance. Be mindful of how rare they are and what a thrill it is to see them. Stand back and observe them and leave them undisturbed as you pass over the HERITAGE TRAIL.

Be especially watchful of desert tortoises. The Fourth Segment passes through areas where they thrive. They are very active in the spring months and during the summer rains. They are difficult to see on the road. You must think "tortoise" to be sure you don't hit one. Do not pick them up as they may become startled and void their bodily fluids -- to your disadvantage! In dry seasons this might cause their death.

The HERITAGE TRAIL would not have been developed without support and interest by BLM officials. The Trail is mostly on public land. BLM is responsible for administering these lands for you and me. They are your agents in this matter, and they approve of the use you're making of the desert. If you travel the HERITAGE TRAIL, drop the BLM people in Needles a note and give them your views on this use of the desert. Better still, stop at their offices to see them if you have an opportunity. They need to know the public is using the Trail, and they need to know what aspects of the experience you benefitted from or enjoyed the most. Also, it would help if you report to BLM any irregularities or problems you've observed while driving the EAST MOJAVE HERITAGE TRAIL.

TED JENSEN

31.

EXPLANATION OF MAPS

   The course of the HERITAGE TRAIL can be seen on the map of the East Mojave Desert on the following page. The small rectangles on that map show the location of the detailed maps that are reproduced on the indicated pages in this Guide. The detailed maps are sandwiched in with the text of this book so that each map precedes the section of narrative with which it is associated. The following are the symbols used on the detailed maps.

LEGEND FOR DETAILED MAPS

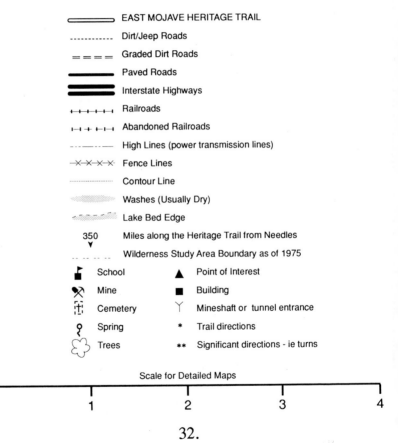

EAST MOJAVE HERITAGE TRAIL

Dirt/Jeep Roads

Graded Dirt Roads

Paved Roads

Interstate Highways

Railroads

Abandoned Railroads

High Lines (power transmission lines)

Fence Lines

Contour Line

Washes (Usually Dry)

Lake Bed Edge

350   Miles along the Heritage Trail from Needles

Wilderness Study Area Boundary as of 1975

School		Point of Interest
Mine		Building
Cemetery		Mineshaft or tunnel entrance
Spring		Trail directions
Trees		Significant directions - ie turns

Scale for Detailed Maps

0   1   2   3   4

EAST MOJAVE DESERT INDEX MAP

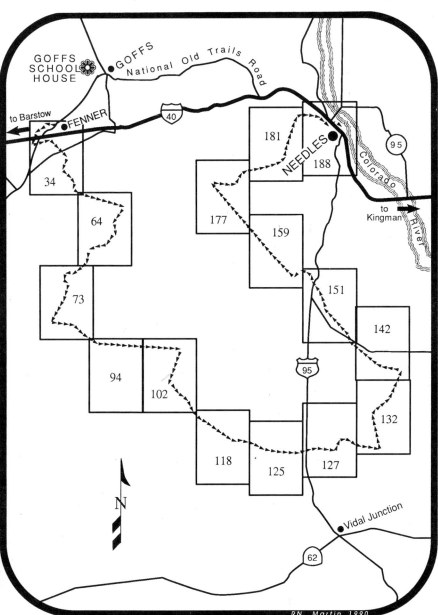

FENNER

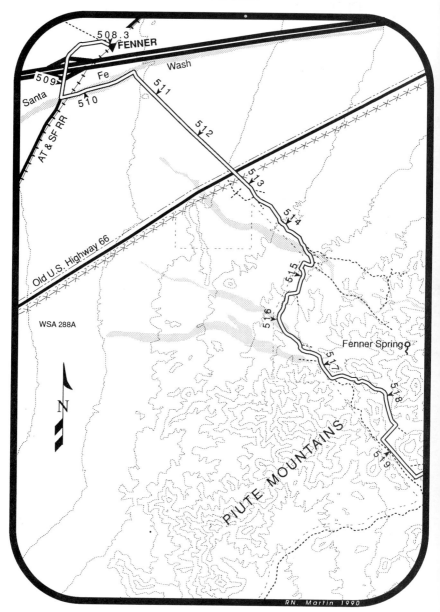

508.3
FENNER
Wash
509
Fe
511
Santa
510
512
AT & SF RR
513
514
Old U.S. Highway 66
515
516
WSA 288A
Fenner Spring
517
518
N
519
PIUTE MOUNTAINS

RN. Martin 1990

GUIDE TO THE EAST MOJAVE HERITAGE TRAIL
FENNER TO SUNFLOWER SPRINGS

This Fourth Segment of the East Mojave Heritage Trail (EMHT) begins at Mile 508.3 at the site of old Fenner on the Santa Fe Railroad and near I-40.

8.3 *   ***   Start at Fenner (site), north of I-40, south of Goffs Road and head northeast. There remains only trees, concrete slabs, and debris at Fenner. Head northwest toward paved Goffs Road (Mile 508.2 on the Third Segment, East Mojave Heritage Trail). We will soon be heading southeast into the Piute Mountains but we must use Goffs Road to get under the freeway. El. 2,096 ft. (0.1).**

8.3   Camping in the wash a few tenths of a mile northwest of Fenner will allow you to observe a typical smoke tree wash community. Plants seen here are the smoke tree, cheesebush, rayless encelia, rattlesnake weed, catclaw acacia, big galleta grass, desert mat, jimpson weed, birdnest buckwheat, black-banded rabbit brush, coyote melon, wire lettuce (desert straw). Some new plants not mentioned in the guide books as yet are the linear-leaved stillingia (*Stillingia linearifolia*) in the spurge family, desert calico (*Loeseliastrum langloisia matthewsii*), in the phlox family, brittle spine-flower (*Chorizanthe brevicornu brevicornu*) in the buckwheat family, mediterranean grass (*Schismus barbatus*), downy dalea (*Dalea mollissima*) in the pea family and the genus that the smoke tree used to reside in. This plant has the glands that are characteristic of this genus, but now all the woody species have been put into the genus *Psorothamnus*

Fenner Motel in the 1920s

Betty (Pettit) Papierski Collection

leaving the annuals in the genus *Dalea*. On the slopes along the wash are creosote bush and burro bush, the indicator species for the creosote bush scrub plant community. Note: When a plant is identified for the first time in this series, the scientific name is given in italics.

.3   FENNER. Prior to the construction of the Nevada Southern Railroad north out of Goffs in 1893, Fenner was the major entry point for the mountain ranges to the south and, more importantly, to much of the region now known as the East Mojave National Scenic Area. The railroad (then Southern Pacific and now Santa Fe) was built in 1883 thereby giving birth to Fenner. Just a short time before, the rich discoveries were made at the Bonanza King and the adjacent town of Providence was booming. Fenner was the shipping point for that region. Also, before the decade of the '80s was over, pioneer ranchers had begun to use the extensive range of the East Mojave. Fenner served as the entrypoint for this activity.

After construction of the Nevada Southern, Goffs became a point of more importance and Fenner began to fade some. However, Fenner managed to hang on over the years. It suffered along with Goffs when Route 66 was realigned in the early 1930s. A post office was maintained in Fenner from February 24, 1892 until September 4, 1970, when it was finally discontinued. There had been a couple of breaks in service during that period. Since 1970 virtually all the buildings in what was once Fenner have been torn down. There is one residence maintained there today.

The following description of Fenner as viewed through the eyes of a small girl was written by Betty (Pettit) Papierski:

You can't work up much excitement when you sa
Fenner these days. It never was the oasis that Goffs wa
But if you lived on the 7IL Ranch, or at Mitchells, o
were a miner, prospector, stranded tourist or out c
tobacco cowboy, Fenner shone like a star.

Fenner had a railroad station depot, some lovel
big cottonwood trees, a postoffice, and small hotel and
store of sorts. Also a gas pump and auto supplies.

You headed to Fenner for the mail. That was reall
important, along with any current news, gossip of hai
raising tales.

You really needed Fenner if you had to use
telephone, it was the only one for miles around. You wer
to Fenner to register and to vote.

True it was a stepping stone to Goffs, Needles, o
Essex, but it was more than that if it was 105° in th
shade and your car or truck had run out of oil, or broke
down, you could walk the miles to Fenner but no farther
Cold pop, beer, or water was there to quench your thirsi

No, Fenner wasn't much, only a vital lifeline,
link to people, a solution in an emergency, and most c
all to two little girls it was that wondrous place where yo
could buy candy.

Betty Papierski has written more of he
recollections of this region and the way it was when sh
lived here in the '20s and early '30s. Her writings o
recollections of the 7IL Ranch are wonderful. An extrac
from those writings is included in the Appendix on page
194 through 200.

**508.4 *   *   (Mile 508.2, Third Segment) Turn lef
(southwest) on paved Goffs Road. This is the poin**

Mark Pettit on "Silver" at 7IL Ranch.
Pettit's Well in Round Valley
is named for him.

1931
Betty (Pettit) Papierski Collection

Goffs Schoolhouse against a late winter sky
braces itself for a new life.

18 March 1990
Dennis Casebier Photo

In 1982 the old Goffs Schoolhouse was about to succumb
to the efforts of vandals.
Jim and Bertha Wold
stepped in. Through a
personal commitment of resources,
energy, and talent, they
saved the old building.
Thanks to Jim and Bertha Wold.

5 January 1990
Dennis Casebier Photo

41.

where a side trip can be made to Goffs Schoolhouse. **El. 2,090 ft. (0.7).**

SIDE TRIP TO GOFFS SCHOOLHOUSE

At Mile 508.4 turn right (northeast) and drive 10 miles on the Goffs Road to visit the community of Goffs and to the Goffs Schoolhouse. The Schoolhouse will be on the left facing Lanfair Road. You can spot it by its flagpole 30 feet tall. The Goffs Cafe and gas station is on across the tracks immediately on the left. The Goffs Schoolhouse is the headquarters of the *Friends of the Mojave Road* and it is being converted into a museum and library focusing on the East Mojave. To continue on the Trail, return by the route you just took to Mile 508.4 and continue southwest on Goffs Road.

END OF SIDE TRIP

509.1 *   **Pass under I-40 westbound. El. 2,050 ft. (0.1).**

509.2 *   **Pass under I-40 eastbound. El. 2,050 ft. (0.4).**

509.6 *   *   Turn left (east) off of paved Goffs Road, up a large channelled wash. This is the point where a side trip can be made to Camp Clipper. El. 2,030 ft. (0.1).

**CAUTION!
GROUPS SHOULD TAKE
CARE IN TURNING LEFT AS
HIGH SPEED TRAFFIC DOES NOT EXPECT
SLOW CROSS TRAFFIC.
CAUTION!**

A group of *Friends of the Mojave Road*
along one of the stone-lined walkways of Camp Clipper.
24 November 1989
Dennis Casebier Photo

Walk quietly and respectfully through the
rows of stones at Camp Clipper.
Observe but do not disturb.
Young Americans came here to the desert.
Blacks and whites by the thousands.
They were young men who had not yet
tasted the full joy of life.
They endured the hardships here
and then went on to endure the horrors of War.
Many did not come back.
Walk quietly and then leave the camp as you found it.

43.

(above) A tiny button (the size of a dime) bearing Army insignia lays on the ground at Camp Clipper.

(right) Jo Ann Smith discovered a cache of artifacts someone had accumulated and then left at Camp Clipper.

24 November 1989
Dennis Casebier Photos

Remains of the World War II airfield
that served Camp Clipper.
It is situated near Essex, California.

3 May 1990
Dennis Casebier Photo

Vince Brunasso Pilot

SIDE TRIP TO CAMP CLIPPER
WITH STOP AT WORLD WAR II AIRFIELD

Camp Clipper was one of the major camps of the World War II Desert Training Center. A history of the Desert Training Center and Camp Clipper by Ev Hayes is given in the Appendix on pages 201 through 223.

0.0   At Mile 509.6 continue ahead (southwest) on paved Goffs Road.

2.8   To visit World War II Airfield, turn right (west) on good dirt road. Railroad signal tower on left on railroad track. Go in 0.5 miles to old runway of Clipper Air Field. Return the 0.5 miles back to Goffs Road and continue southwest toward Essex.

4.2   Reach "Route 66" (now erroneously marked "National Trails Highway") and turn right.

5.9   Essex, California. Turn right on Essex Road (northwest toward Mitchell's Caverns and I-40).

8.4   Turn right off Essex Road onto dirt road. CAMP CLIPPER. Rock alignments on both sides of road. There are many roadways, rock alignments, and other signs of the old army camp. To continue on the trail, return by the route you just took to Mile 509.6 and turn right (east) up the large wash.

END OF SIDE TRIP

509.7 *   **Pass under railroad bridge 619.6. El. 2,040 ft.**
(0.7).

A history of the Santa Fe Railway by Delmer G. Ross is given in the Appendix on pages 224 through 237.

510.4 *   **Bear to right of wash to bypass rough bedrock. El. 2,100 ft. (0.3).**

510.4   Rayless encelia, wire lettuce, black-banded rabbit brush, smoke tree, cheesebush, coyote melon, and the desert mat and downy dalea can be seen on the wash floor forming mat-like patches. A quick smell of the foliage will separate the two quite easily. The dalea will have the small glands and quite a pungent odor.

510.7 *   ***   Turn right (south) out of wash over bank and bear right shortly after crest to join a once graded road. El. 2,110 ft. (0.0+).**

510.7+   ****   Turn left (southeast) on once graded road. El. 2,110 ft. (0.2).**

510.7+   Out of the wash on the alluvial fan the vegetation is composed of plant species associated with the creosote bush scrub plant community where it occurs at higher elevations in the Mojave Desert. Along with the two indicator species of this community, cheesebush, Mojave yucca, pencil cholla, buckhorn cholla, golden/silver cholla, barrel cactus, krameria (*Krameira parvifolia*), and inflated buckwheat can be observed in the next two miles of the Trail.

510.9 *   **A rounded hill 50 feet high is immediately on your right. El. 2,140 ft. (1.8).**

2.7 *   **Cross under a wooden pole line. El. 2,320 ft. (0.0+).**

2.7   DESERT TORTOISE. Perhaps the most loved of all desert creatures is the California State Reptile, the desert tortoise. He is completely inoffensive. He eats only vegetable matter and he is the only desert animal that can be approached by man with impunity. He makes no effort to escape other than retreating into his shell.

Unfortunately, in recent years the numbers of desert tortoises seems to have decreased to the point that some consider the species to be threatened. The Fourth Segment of the East Mojave Heritage Trail passes through significant desert tortoise habitat. It is important that you understand the lifestyle of these wonderful animals so that you will not inadvertently negatively impact him in any way.

It is disastrous to the desert tortoise to pick him up and especially to yield to the temptation to take one home. It is against the law and it will almost certainly result in harm to the tortoise. The best rule is to watch and study them, photograph them to your heart's content, but do not even touch one. Although, there may be times when it is wise to remove one from the roadway in cases where he is likely to be hit.

The desert tortoise has a number of enemies. Many are killed on roads, although largely that happens on high speed roads and not on the backcountry byways. Instances of ravens preying on young tortoises have been observed and the number of ravens living in desert areas is believed to have increased dramatically over the past few decades. Diseases have hit the tortoises hard in recent years. These diseases may have been introduced into healthy

DESERT TORTOISE
The California State Reptile
Observe, photograph, and admire him from a
distance. Then let him go his way
untouched and unbothered by you.

1 June 1990
Dennis Casebier Photo

populations by tortoises that had been in captivity being released into the wild. The problems with diseases and reduction in numbers in general are especially bad in the Western Mojave Desert. Populations in the East Mojave continue to appear viable and healthy, even though we are in the midst of a bad drought.

Be tortoise conscious as you drive through the backcountry of the East Mojave. Commit no depredation against the tortoise and report to BLM any misconduct or violations that come within the scope of your personal observations.

When the white man first came to this country, desert tortoises were relatively scarce because they were hunted relentlessly by the Indians. In a land where food was hard to find, the tortoise provided a ready-made meal. The following article on this subject appeared in a newspaper on April 22, 1893: *The land turtles of the Mohave desert prove an edible dish to the tribes of Indians who infest that region when cooked in a savory style. The turtle, when captured, is placed on its back on a bed of hot coals and cooked, the basin-like shell retaining all the meat and gravey. When done to a turn the shell forming the under part of the turtle is removed and the feast is ready for the guests.*

512.7+   ******   **Cross paved road which is the last alignment of U.S. Highway 66 and the flood control berm in 100 feet. Continue southeast up gradual slope toward Piute Mountains on lesser, ungraded road. El. 2,320 ft. (0.4).**

**CAUTION!
THIS PAVED ROAD IS THE FORMER
U.S.HIGHWAY 66.
TRAVELERS ON IT WILL BE OPERATING AT
HIGHWAY SPEEDS
AND THEY WILL NOT BE EXPECTING
SLOW CROSS TRAFFIC.
CAUTION!**

513.1 * ***** **"Y." Bear right (straight -- southeast) toward mountains. El. 2,350 ft. (0.1).**

513.2 * **Intersect road coming in from right and continue southeast along top of ridge. Trail will shortly enter Piute Mountains. El. 2,360 ft. (0.1).**

513.2 Annuals such as the woolly plantain (*Plantago fastigiata*), rigid spiny-herb, and the desert sunflower are on the slopes where the desert pavement occurs. The perennial desert senna in the pea family will be quite obvious if in bloom as its brilliant yellow flowers are quite showy.

513.3 * ***** **"Y." Bear left (southeast) slightly uphill on top of rounded ridge. El. 2,400 ft. (1.0).**

GEOLOGY ALONG THE 4TH SEGMENT
The various segments of the East Mojave Heritage Trail differ greatly in their historical background and in the natural features along the way. It was geologist Steven Pencall who stated: "Nature takes the center stage on the Fourth Segment." That is very true. Part of the cause is that there is less human history in this Segment than in the

Rockhounding is a popular pastime in the East Mojave.

more elevated country of the East Mojave touched by the other three Segments. Another factor in highlighting nature on the Fourth Segment is that the geology of the country is wonderfully exposed. We have had the advantage of having two geologists write material for this Guide -- Steve Pencall and Jim Vernon. Their observations are sandwiched in at the appropriate spots throughout the book. At the end of the material provided by Steve we've ended each entry with a "SP." The material provided by Jim is indicated with a "JV."

In addition to the site-specific descriptions, Steve Pencall has prepared an "Introduction to the Geology of the Fourth Segment of the East Mojave Heritage Trail" which is reproduced in the Appendix on pages 238 through 240. I recommend that you take the time to read that overview early in the trip.

513.3   You are now climbing an old alluvial fan surface which has younger ravines being cut into it as renewed uplift of the Piute Mountains has increased the erosive power of the streams that traverse it. In crossing the Piute Mountains from northwest to southeast we will see that they consist of a small sliver of volcanic rocks on the northwest with the core of the range made up of a variable mixture of metamorphic rocks which in turn has been intruded by several granitic rock bodies. SP.

513.3   As the Piute Mountains are entered this is as good a time as any to review the general geology of the East Mojave: a series of medium to small mountain ranges, generally trending northwest to southeast, separated by elongated basins or valleys. The mountain building has occurred as a result of two geologic events. First, the

54.

orogeny may be traced to a series of fault lines along which blocks of old rocks have been elevated and the basins between the parallel or nearly parallel fault lines have either remained stationary or been downdropped. Second, the mountains are the result of recent geologic volcanism, some 30 or 60 million years ago, with magma (liquid rock below the surface) welling up along fault lines in great volumes. Since the time of these methods of mountain building, the adjoining basins have become filled with alluvial (alluvium) depositions, thus creating the flattish valley floors (bajadas) and the "drowning" of the mountain mass in its own rock debris.

The Piute Mountains are a good example of fault-block mountains, and (as the traveler proceeds a little farther) are represented by some of the oldest rock on this segment -- being Precambrian in age (about 1.8 to 2.4 billion years of age). The basement granite has been thrust up along two nearly parallel fault lines. JV.

4.3 *   *   **"Y." Bear right (southeast) downhill. El. 2,410 ft. (0.0+).**

4.3   Beavertail cactus and hedgehog cactus on the slopes of the Piute Mountains.

4.3   Small hill on left (east) composed of a pinkish-gray volcanic rock called welded tuff (sometimes called ignimbrite), which was formed by a cloud of volcanic fragments from dust-sized to fist-sized or larger that were so hot they fused together upon settling to the ground. Welded tuff of various compositions is encountered at several locations along the Fourth Segment. SP.

Be forewarned!
The elevation on the Fourth Segment
is lower on the average than the first three
Segments of the East Mojave Heritage Trail.
Summer temperatures can be much higher.

4.3+ * Continue ahead (southeast). Ignore road left up wash. El. 2,410 ft. (0.2).

4.3+ Nevada Mormon tea on slopes descending from the pass with desert senna in the drainage courses.

4.5 * Continue ahead (south). Ignore road left. El. 2,590 ft. (0.1).

4.6 * * **"T." Turn right (west) downhill. Trail will soon turn south. This is the point where a side trip can be made to Fenner Spring. El. 2,600 ft. (0.4).**

SIDE TRIP TO FENNER SPRING

0.0 At Mile 514.6 turn left (southeast) uphill.

0.1 Road enters, and goes up wash.

0.1+ Turn right off once graded road to continue up wash.

0.2 "Y." Bear left (southeast) to go up left branch of wash.

0.3 Contact between tuff and gray marble to right (southwest). Hot solutions given off when the volcanic rocks were still hot carried iron minerals into the marble which has weathered rusty-brown along the contact. Such contacts are often favorable places to look for minerals and mineral assessment work has been done along the contact across the wash to the north. SP.

Left-to-right
Mr. Meulhisen, Mark Pettit, and two
Los Angeles men.
They had been inspecting a mine
near Fenner Spring.

Late 1920s
Betty (Pettit) Papierski Collection

0.4   Remains of old mining camp on right of wash.

0.6   Remains of old mining camp on right of wash.

1.0   Dark augen gneiss, (pronounced "nice") a type of metamorphic rock, exposed in hill on left (north). Augens (German: eyes) are the oval patches of white quartz. Gneiss is exposed along the rest of the trail to Fenner Spring. SP.

1.4   Turn right (southeast) up side wash over buried steel water tank six feet in diameter.

1.9   Park at wide spot in wash near railroad tie post and walk up canyon (south) 0.3 miles to two fenced enclosures containing the springs. Do not camp here or pollute the water. To continue on the Trail, return by the route you just took to Mile 514.6 and continue downhill (west).

For about a year in the 1920s Charlie and Elizabeth Hammond lived with their family at a site along the Trail to Fenner Spring. The pipe was in place when they went there having been installed many years earlier by the railroad. They repaired it and piped the water down to their home site. During that period their children, Charlie Jr., Lenna, and Lillian, attended school at Goffs. Charlie drove himself and the other children to school in a Model T. They had quite a long drive over an unimproved road down to the old alignment of Route 66. Later the Hammonds owned land and had a service station along the present alignment of old Route 66. They raised cattle also. They moved to a better site near Hiko Springs

59.

not far from the present Laughlin, Nevada.

A prospector and mine promoter named Meulhisen frequented this area at the time. Hammond family stories relate how Meulhisen used to load his shotgun with gold and blast it into the face of barren rock when prospective investors came out to inspect. He sold lots of claims.

END OF SIDE TRIP

515.0 * ***** **"Y." Bear right (southwest) on the better road. El. 2,630 ft. (0.9).**

515.1+ Saddle. Contact between quartzite (metamorphosed sandstone) on left (east) and welded tuff. When a geologic contact occurs in a saddle, it often indicates that the contact is a fault since erosion proceeds more rapidly in the shattered rocks along the fault. SP.

515.9 * ***** **Trail goes south into mountains. El. 2,690 ft. (0.4).**

516.3 * ***** **"Y." Bear right (straight -- south). El. 2,770 ft. (0.3).**

516.3 Fine-grained gray limestone on hill to left (east) similar to limestone at the Bonanza King Mine in the Providence Mountains. Limestone slopes are often poorly vegetated due to the alkaline soil. SP.

516.6 * **Continue ahead (southeast). Ignore road coming in from right rear. El. 2,830 ft. (0.3).**

16.6   Green Mormon tea, goldeneye, bladder sage, buckhorn cholla, golden/silver cholla, barrel cactus, and hedgehog cactus on slopes in this area.

16.9 *   **Trail is going south up scenic canyon 200 feet wide. El. 2,890 ft. (0.3).**

16.9   Woolly brickelbush, California buckwheat, goldeneye, barrel cactus, desert senna, bladder sage, linear-leaved stillingia, black-banded rabbit brush, California buckwheat, cheesebush, catclaw acacia with the hemiparasite California mistletoe, Mojave yucca, another species of *krameria,* white ratney (*Krameria grayii*) and the more southern ranging agave will occur on the slopes and in the washes along this section of the Trail. The two species of *krameria* are easily separated if you have the fruit. *K. grayii* has barbs only at the tip of the spines on the fruit while *K. parrifolia* has them along the length of the spine. A hand magnifying glass is helpful as to the eye the fruit of both appear as small sputniks. A third species of Mormon tea, California Mormon tea occurs here and is identifiable from the other two species in this area as it has three leaves. The other two have only two leaves at the nodes on the stems.

17.2 * *   **"Y." Bear left (east) into side canyon on left that will soon bear right. El. 2,950 ft. (0.8).**

17.5   Canyon cut into gray and pink limestone. Century plants (agave) often show preference for limestone. SP.

18.0 *   **Surrounded by giant man-eating cholla in a scenic canyon 700 feet wide. El. 3,150 ft. (0.5).**

61.

With Jo Ann Smith and Carl Volkmar in the lead,
a caravan of the
Friends of the Mojave Road
approaches the hill at Mile 518.8.

25 November 1989
Dennis Casebier Photo

8.5 * * **Turn right (southwest) toward low pass on ridge visible 0.3 miles away. El. 3,280 ft. (0.3).**

8.5 An infrequently occurring pungently ill-smelling shrubby perennial, odora (*Porophyllum gracile*) occurs on the rocky slopes and washes in this area as well as goldeneye, desert senna, and California buckwheat.

8.5 Twenty feet high outcrop of massive quartz on left (east) 75 feet shows slickensides -- parallel striations caused by fault movement along the surface. The mountain to the south is composed of an unusual granite which contains two different types of mica. The granite is believed to be of late Cretaceous age -- about 80 million years old. SP.

3.8 * **Crest of ridge. El. 3,360 ft. (0.0+).**

3.8+ ** **Turn left (south) at bottom of ridge to go up canyon we turned out of at Mile 517.2. El. 3,360 ft. (0.1).**

3.9 * **Continue ahead (southeast) on left side of canyon. Benchmark T8N-32/R18E-38/T7N-5/R18E-4 on right 20 feet. El. 3,350 ft. (0.4).**

0.1 We are traveling along the contact between the granite and dark gray mica schist (a metamorphic rock) to the south. The line of weakness along which the canyon is formed may be a fault -- now buried under the sand. SP.

0.3 * **Top of small rise. Continue ahead (south) going**

BURNING SHOE WASH

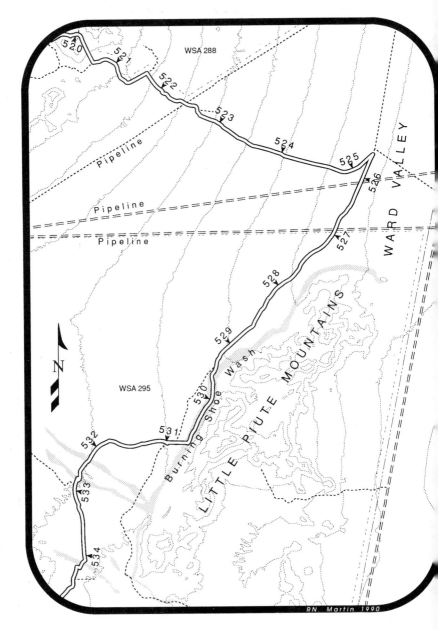

520
521
WSA 288
522
523
524
525
526
WARD VALLEY
Pipeline
Pipeline
Pipeline
527
528
529
530
531
532
533
534
WSA 295
N
Burning Shoe Wash
LITTLE PIUTE MOUNTAINS
RN. Martin 1990

up canyon. Ignore short dead end road left. El. 3,450 ft. (0.3).

).3   At this location are seen some unusually sculptured rock formations: highly fractured -- looking for all the world as if one has been at work with a massive ruler creating many vertical lines or fractures. While the formations appear to be stacks of rocks, fingers, or totems, they are in reality highly weathered granite with most of the rock breakdown being accomplished by chemical weathering. Many of the fracture lines have weathered sufficiently so that feldspar clay (from the weathering of the granite) has filled in the fractures further highlighting the "ruler" effect. JV.

9.6 *   Trail bears left (northeast) at head of canyon as it opens into a small valley. This valley with the island of rock in the center 300 feet high is the southernmost range of the Mojave Road Toad, *Bufo Casebieris*, an endangered species. El. 3,530 ft. (0.1).

9.7 *   *   "Y." Bear right (straight -- east) to join the road coming in from right rear that circles the island of rock. The Trail circles half way around island clockwise. El. 3,560 ft. (0.2).

9.9 *   Pass between boulder piles. Island of rock is on your right. El. 3,630 ft. (0.1).

0.0 *   *   "Y." Bear right (east) to continue circling island of rock clockwise. Road left goes 0.4 of a mile to a scenic overview of the canyon we left at Mile 518.8. El. 3,690 ft. (0.0+).

520.0   For a closer inspection of these weathered grani
rock structures mentioned at Mile 519.3, take the sho
side trip of 0.4 miles to the scenic overview of tl
canyon. JV.

**520.0+   *   Continue ahead (southeast). Ignore road le
that comes in from scenic overview. El. 3,690 ft. (0.5**

**520.5 *   *   "T." Turn left (east) to shortly go downhill an
leave Bufo Valley behind. El. 3,560 ft. (0.6).**

**521.1 *   Continue ahead (southeast) down slight slope c
Piute Mountains. Ignore faint road left. El. 3,450 f
(0.3).**

521.1   In descending from the Piute Mountains at th
point, the Trail traverses the upper regions of the bajad
of the adjoining basin or valley. This portion of the bajad
is commonly known as the pediment section of th
alluvium-filled basin. Lower segments of this range ar
being buried by the rock debris -- these are the famou
inselbergs of desert landscapes (so-called because whe
first studied in other deserts they reminded the geologi
observer of islands or icebergs sticking out of a "frozen
sea). JV.

521.4 *   Leaving mountains behind. El. 3,360 ft. (0.2)

521.6 *   *   "Y." Bear right (southeast). El. 3,310 ft. (0.8)

521.6   You are looking across Ward Valley at severa
mountain ranges of very complex geologic structure. I
the foreground at 12:30 (with 12:00 being straight ahead

3:00 being to the right, etc.) are the Little Piute Mountains with the dark western front of the Stepladder Mountains just visible behind the Little Piutes. The Sacramento Mountains near the end of the Fourth Segment are at 9:30 while the light-colored dome at 10:30 is the saddle between the Sacramentos and the Chemehuevi Mountains to the south. The geology of each range will be discussed as they are traversed or closely approached. SP.

522.1   Cottontop cactus appears on slopes and alluvial fan and big galleta grass becomes more common.

522.4 *   *   **Cross gas line road which can be seen extending left across Ward Valley to disappear 16 miles away near Flattop Mountain. Continue southeast. Eagle Mountain can be seen to the right of Flattop Mountain at a distance of 16 miles at about 10:30. The Stepladder Mountains are about 14 miles away at one o'clock. The Little Piutes are 5 miles away at two o'clock and behind them on the horizon are the Turtle Mountains. Homer Wash, five miles ahead is a major drain for Ward Valley which stretches out left and right in front of you. El. 3,110 ft. (0.2).**

522.4   You are passing over an underground pipe called the Four Corners Pipeline. The line runs from Red Mesa, Utah to Long Beach, California carrying crude oil from the fields in Utah to the refineries in California. It is a 16-inch pipe covered with a minimum (usually) of three feet of dirt. The pipeline crosses ravines where it is not covered at all. It was constructed in 1957 and has operated more or less continuously since that time. It is

Desert Wildlife

This is the deadly Mojave Green Rattlesnake.
Give him much respect and a wide berth.
Do not kill or in any way bother any of the
critters of the desert. They are a natural
part of this environment. Many of them are
secretive and are seldom seen. Many are fierce
and some are dangerous. It is the way of the desert.

Please read the vignettes on Wildlife by
Mike McGill in the Appendix
on pages 241 through 270.

18 October 1980
Dennis Casebier Photo

68.

the same pipeline crossed at Mile 21.0 on the First Segment of the East Mojave Heritage Trail.

2.6 *   *   **"Y." Bear right (south). El. 3,050 ft. (2.7).**

5.3 *   **Trail bears slightly left to head east toward Eagle Mountain 13 miles away on horizon. El. 2,360 ft. (0.3).**

5.6 *   *   **Turn hard right, almost 180°, (southwest) 200 feet before reaching a right angle intersection. We will stay on this road for 3.9 miles. El. 2,340 ft. (0.5).**

6.1 *   **Continue ahead (southwest) across graded road. El. 2,340 ft. (0.8).**

DESERT WILDLIFE. Very little has been said in the Guides to the East Mojave Heritage Trail about wildlife. This is largely because wildlife moves around and the Guides are designed to point out objects and plants that are fixed on the ground. And yet the wildlife of the desert is one of its greatest attractions and a source of fascination to those who frequent the backcountry. To alleviate this hiatus, wildlife biologist Mike McGill has prepared an overview statement of desert wildlife and brief sketches that describe some of the most commonly encountered species. This information is reproduced in the Appendix on pages 241 through 270.

6.9 *   **Cross gas line raised berm. El. 2,390 ft. (0.0+).**

6.9+   *   **Cross gas line road and pass under wooden pole line. El. 2,390 ft. (0.2).**

527.1 *　　　　Little Piute Mountains are parallel to Trail left 0.3 miles. El. 2,400 ft. (0.4).

527.5 *　　　　Old Woman Statue visible ahead (southwest) slightly left 14 miles away on crest of Old Woman Mountains. El. 2,440 ft. (1.8).

527.5　　　　The Little Piute Mountains are essentially a repetition of the geologic sequence observed in the Piute Mountains -- not surprising since they are believed to have slid away from the Piute Mountains down a detachment fault -- rotating slightly clockwise in the process. We can see volcanic rocks such as rhyolite and welded tuffs along the west face of the range, but we do not see the metamorphic and granitic rocks on the east side of the range. SP.

529.3 *　*　　　Continue ahead (southwest). Ignore tracks left and right. El. 2,630 ft. (0.2).

CAUTION!

The soft sand wash starting at Mile 529.5 is 1.3 miles long and 4WD vehicles have become stuck or overheated traveling through it. It should not be traversed alone as this is a very remote section of the Mojave Desert. Experienced drivers reduce their tire pressure in terrain like this to provide more traction.

CAUTION!

529.5 *　*　　　Turn left (south) into sand wash (this is the famous Burning Shoe Wash), then right to continue in the same direction, southwest, alongside Little Piute Mountains on your left. El. 2,650 ft. (0.2).

The East Mojave Heritage Trail
showing the soft sand near Mile 530.

If the sand is damp, it will be firm and will
provide a good base for driving. If it has
been hot and dry, however, then the sand
will be soft and even a 4WD can get
stuck or "temporarily detained."

25 November 1989
Dennis Casebier Photo

529.5   Cottontop cactus on rocky outcrops along wash well as krameria, California Mormon tea, bladder sag desert senna, desert almond with its associated te catapillars and desert marigold in the wash. The dese milkweed (*Asclepias erosa*) can also be seen in the wa with its large leaves and milky sap. Many desert insee can be seen visiting these plants.

529.7 *   Continue south in wash. Ignore road left. I 2,660 ft. (0.1).

529.8 *   *   "Y." Bear left (southwest). Trail (wash) narro and goes left alongside mountain. El. 2,670 ft. (0.1

529.9 *   *   "Y." Bear left (southwest). Trail (wash) narro and goes left alongside mountain. El. 2,680 ft. (0.1

530.0 *   *   Monument (Cairn) 10 feet left on bank mar a place where a pair of honest shoes were burned 30 December 1984. Continue ahead (southwest) in sa wash. El. 2,690 ft. (0.8).

530.1   Welded rhyolite tuff exposed in bank of wash left (east) capped by a cliff-forming welded tuff at the t of the hill. The vertical joints in the tuff were formed contraction as the rock cooled. SP.

530.8 *   *   Turn right (west) out of sand wash away fre mountains. El. 2,750 ft. (0.2).

531.0 *   *   Trail joins road we left at Mile 529.5 ar continues west. El. 2,770 ft. (0.1).

OLD WOMAN STATUE

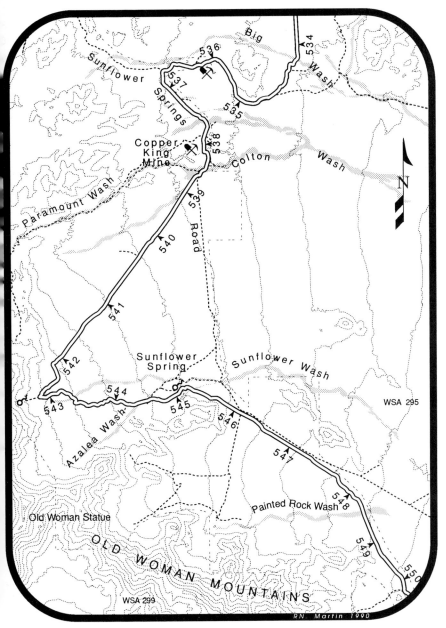

Alan Siebert beside his Land Rover *RINO*
with a caravan taking a break on the
East Mojave Heritage Trail
near Mile 532.

25 November 1989
Dennis Casebier Photo

| 531.1 * | * | "Y." Bear right (northwest). El. 2,790 ft. (0.3). |

531.1 * * "Y." Bear right (northwest). El. 2,790 ft. (0.3).

531.4 * * "Y." Bear left (straight -- west). El. 2,810 ft. (0.9).

532.3 * * Cross well vegetated wash eight feet deep and 100 feet wide and continue southwest. El. 2,820 ft. (0.4).

532.7 * Cross well vegetated wash 50 feet wide and continue southwest. El. 2,790 ft. (0.1).

532.8 * Cross deep wash 10 feet wide and continue southwest. El. 2,820 ft. (0.1).

532.9 * Crest of small hill. Old Woman Statue visible ahead 9 miles away on horizon. Turtle Mountains visible across Ward Valley at 10:30, 8 miles away. El. 2,820 ft. (1.2).

533.1 Welded tuff exposed on top of hill at mile 530.1 is at ground level on left (east). SP.

534.1 * Cross Big Wash 50 feet wide and continue southwest. El. 2,790 ft. (0.4).

534.5 * * "Y." Bear right to intersect a road and continue southwest. El. 2,810 ft. (0.3).

534.8 * * Intersect a road coming in from left rear, bearing right to continue southwest. El. 2,850 ft. (0.6).

535.2 Hills on right (north) are mostly granitic rocks

with scattered welded tuff and other volcanics. These hill are blocks that were originally attached to the Old Woma: Mountains but became detached as the Little Piutes move into their present position. SP.

535.4 *   **Continue ahead (north). Ignore road enterin, from right rear. El. 2,950 ft. (0.7).**

535.7   Sliver of limestone exposed in hill on right (north) SP.

536.1 *   **Continue ahead (west) past point of rock witl mine up on side of hill left. El. 3,040 ft. (0.1).**

536.1   Paperflower occurs and prince's plume with its ta stalk-like yellow flowering parts.

536.2 *   *****   **"Y." Bear left (west) on main road. El. 3,050 ft (0.1).**

536.3 *   **Continue ahead (west). Ignore crossroad. E 3,050 ft. (0.4).**

536.7 *   **Continue ahead (southwest). Ignore road right El. 3,050 ft. (0.0+).**

536.7+   ******   **"Y." Bear left (straight, west). El. 3,050 ft (0.1).**

536.8 *   *****   **"T." Turn left (south) on well used Sunflowe Springs Road. We will stay on this road for the nex 1.9 miles. Ignore the several lesser roads crossing. Thi is the point where a side trip can be made to Willov Spring. El. 3,130 ft. (0.5).**

SIDE TRIP TO WILLOW SPRING

0.0   At Mile 536.8 turn right (north) on well graded Sunflower Springs Road.

1.7   "Y." Turn left (northwest).

2.3   "Y." Turn right (northwest).

2.5   Ignore road left to windmill (Weaver's Well). Continue ahead (northwest).

2.5+   Ignore road left to windmill. Continue ahead (northwest).

2.6+   Intersection, turn left and cross wide graded road and in 50 feet, intersect (bearing half right) and join a road going northwest.

2.7   Continue ahead (west). Ignore road coming in from right rear.

3.0   Continue ahead across sand wash 40 feet wide.

3.1   Continue ahead (southwest). Ignore road left.

3.2   Mine tailings left and right.

4.2   Continue ahead (southwest). Ignore road right.

4.6   Continue ahead (south). Ignore road right.

4.9   Continue ahead (south). Ignore road left.

5.3   "Y." Bear right (south).

5.4   "Y." Bear right (south).

6.3   "T." Turn left up sand wash 40 feet wide.

6.8   Turn right (northwest) immediately after passing water tank, corral and stone barn.

7.1   Road turns left (southwest) into scenic valley with juniper, cholla, and yucca.

7.2   Continue ahead (southwest) up left side of valley. Ignore road right.

7.5   Continue ahead (southwest). Road gets rougher.

7.6   Road crosses wash which has 100 feet of white bedrock in bottom, usually with water (not much in it from spring upstream a few hundred feet. Road continues up far bank and then goes right to a camping spot. To continue on the Trail, return by the route you just took to Mile 536.8 and continue south on Sunflower Springs Road.

END OF SIDE TRIP

537.3 *   **Continue ahead (southeast) just after crossing vegetated wash. El. 3,050 ft. (0.3).**

537.6 *   **Cross wash 15 feet deep. Continue ahead (southeast). El. 3,020 ft. (0.2).**

(above) A caravan approaches the Old Woman Mountains.
(below) The Old Woman Statue.
Dennis Casebier Photos

537.8 *   **Cross wash 25 feet deep. Continue ahead (south). Ignore tracks down wash. El. 3,000 ft. (0.1).**

537.9 *   **Continue ahead (southwest). Ignore road coming in from left rear. El. 3,030 ft. (0.1).**

538.0 *   **Continue ahead (southwest). Ignore road right to mine and road left. El. 3,030 ft. (0.1).**

538.1 *   **Continue ahead (southwest). Ignore road left. El. 3,020 ft. (0.2).**

538.3 *   **Cross wash 20 feet deep and continue south. Ignore road left just before wash. El. 2,990 ft. (0.1).**

538.4 *   **"Y." Bear right (southwest). El. 3,010 ft. (0.1).**

538.5 *   **Cross Colton Wash which is 40 feet deep. Ignore road left just before wash. El. 3,000 ft. (0.2).**

538.7 *   *   **Turn half-right (southwest) off Sunflower Springs Road after crossing Colton Wash and climbing bank. There is a large cairn at this point. Trail goes up a slight slope on a well defined road. El. 3,050 ft. (0.5).**

538.7   The origin of the Old Woman Mountains is basically that of fault-blocking, with the main ridge of the range being Precambrian granite. The "statue" is really another one of those totems or fingers, seen at Mile 519.3. It appears that about the geologic time the uplifting of the very old granite began to occur, movement along the fault lines released pressure below the surface. Magma was formed and began to rise along the fault lines, hence, the appearance of Tertiary volcanics. JV.

38.7   We are indebted to Needles pioneer Charles Battye for the information that the name "Old Woman Mountains" is of Indian origin. In a note to *Desert Magazine* (December 1940, p.36) he states as follows: "This range [Old Woman Mountains], southeast of Danby, on U. S. Highway 66, was so named by the Pahute and Chemehuevi Indians, who are identical in race and language. They called it *No-mop'-wits*, which means literally 'old woman.' There can be seen, from a certain point of view, a tall, columnar rock, and monolith which bears a resemblance to the form of an old woman." The Old Woman Statue, as it is now called, is visible along here and off and on for the next several miles along the Trail. See photograph on page 79.

39.2 *   Trail gets sandy. El. 3,130 ft. (1.1).

40.3 *   Continue ahead (southwest). Ignore road right. El. 3,310 ft. (1.9).

40.3   Granodiorite boulders (an igneous rock similar to granite) on either side of road. Junipers begin to appear. We reached this elevation in the Piute Mountains, yet saw no junipers even on slopes well above this elevation. Why? The Old Womans are higher than the Piutes and receive more precipitation on the highest slopes but perhaps more important is the role the "heat sink" effect the larger mass of the Old Woman Mountains plays in moderating the extremes of climate. At comparable

81.

elevations the Old Womans stay cool longer into the summer and warm longer into the winter. SP.

542.2 *   **Surrounded by scenic rock garden and juniper trees. Trail has turned left slightly to go south. El. 3,830 ft. (0.6).**

542.2   Cheesebush, bladder sage, goldeneye, California buckwheat, boxthorn, inflated buckwheat, mound cactus, pencil cholla, golden/silver cholla, and felt thorn or Mojave horsebrush are found in this area. A different brickellbush, the narrowleaf brickellbush (*Brickellia oblongifolia linifolia*) in the cracks of the boulders in this area and Mojave rattleweed (*Astragalus mohavensis mohavensis*) on the flat areas along the Trail can also be observed.

542.2   The "rock garden" is the weathered segments of exposed Precambrian granite. Note that as the granite weathers, very coarse light colored sand is produced. As in the case of any exposed outcroppings of rock, the desert winds play a role in the sculpturing of these structures, but they are really not ventifacts (wind weathered rocks). JV.

542.8 *   *****   **"T." Turn hard left (east), downhill. Do not go right toward inhabited cabins visible against mountain. El. 3,990 ft. (1.6).**

543.0   Dike on left (south) in wash is a pegmatite, a coarse-grained rock of quartz and feldspar. It contains more quartz than the surrounding granodiorite. SP.

44.4 *   Continue ahead (east). Ignore road right. El. 3,510 ft. (0.1).

44.5 *   Continue ahead (east). Fence line alongside on right. El. 3,480 ft. (0.1).

44.5   Bladderpod in the area among the rocks can be identified by its yellow flowers and pods when in bloom or its deep green foliage when not flowering.

44.6 * *   "Y." Bear right (east) and pass between gate posts of fence. El. 3,450 ft. (0.4).

44.6   Shrubs in the wash are squaw waterweed indicating the presence of water near the surface as this is the drainage that feeds Sunflower Springs. Desert willow (*Chilopsis linearis*) also occurs in this wash system.

45.0 *   Continue ahead (northeast). Ignore faint road right. El. 3,330 ft. (0.1).

45.1 * *   Sunflower Springs area, ranch house, corral left. Continue ahead (east). Ignore roads left to ranch house. El. 3,310 ft. (0.1).

45.1   The springs are basically the result of the aquifer fed by runoff from the Old Woman Mountains being blocked by the granite uplifts that show up as the small hills surrounding the ranch buildings. An aquifer is a strata of rock that has a high ability to hold a liquid, i.e., large numbers of pore spaces between the intervening grains. JV.

(above) The EMHT in the Old Woman Mountains.
(below) One of the old buildings at Sunflower Springs.
Dennis Casebier Photos

We don't know who named Sunflower Springs and we don't know when the first buildings were erected. Certainly both events occurred well back into the 1800s -- probably shortly after the railroad was built in 1883. Walter C. Mendenhall in his book *Routes to Desert Watering Places,* published in 1909, knew of Sunflower Springs and described it as follows: "These springs are on the eastern border of a northern extension of Old Woman Mountain, about 12 miles in an air line southeast of Fenner. The springs are in a cove about half a mile up a canyon which intersects the mountain. There are neither roads nor regular trails to them, but they may be found by the cattle paths that lead to them. The water comes from limestone and is of good quality." This statement not only identifies an early use of the name "Sunflower Springs," it also shows that this range was being used for cattle at least as early as 1909, and probably quite a lot earlier.

The history of the East Mojave centers around the colorful and dynamic people who have lived here. Jim Craig holds his own among the most interesting of the East Mojave oldtimers.

It is believed Jim Craig first came to the East Mojave with his family of five children in 1914. He settled at Barnwell working for the Rock Springs Land & Cattle Company. He was frequently gone out on the vast range working cattle. His children frequently fended for themselves while attending school in Barnwell.

Jim was a loner. Much of the time he lived in isolated corners of the desert by himself. In the early

Jim Craig (right) and Mark Pettit in 1931

Betty (Pettit) Papierski Photo

'20s, as the country was settling into the realities of prohibition, Jim situated himself at Sunflower Springs and pursued the most lucrative business option then available in the desert country -- the manufacture of whiskey. There were already buildings there and it is not likely he added substantially to those buildings at that time.

After living at Sunflower Springs for several years, he moved to the 7IL Ranch when it was owned and operated by Mark Pettit. He worked around the ranch and sort of became part of the family.

In the '30s he was living at Sunflower Springs again -- this time raising cattle. He married Eva Parker of Essex in 1940 and they made their home at Sunflower. During this period he added to the buildings. He commenced operation of the cattle ranch in this region that covered much of the range of today's Lazy Daisy Ranch. Also Jim and Eva raised chukkers at Sunflower Springs that were sold to the Department of Fish and Game for release into the wild in various places in the California Desert.

Jim and Eva lived at Sunflower for many years. After his death the ranch was sold to Harold and Edith Knight and after a few years was abandoned. Jim Craig's daughter Eunice Gallinari attempted to reactivate the old grazing lease without success. She and her son John Bentley had grazed cattle on that range when Jim was still there.

In about 1978 Milton Blair, grandson of the pioneer family of Frank Murphy of Lanfair Valley, moved cattle on to that range, and, although he makes use of water at Sunflower Springs for his cattle, his headquarters are not there. His spread is known as the

Lazy Daisy Ranch. It has been a successful operation for many years.

The land in this region consists of a mixture of private and public lands. The percentage of land in private ownership is particularly high because many sections in the area were deeded to the railroad when the first tracks were built through from Barstow to Needles along what is now the Santa Fe mainline. Original construction was by the Southern Pacific Railroad and therefore some of the land is still owned by Southern Pacific. Much of their original land has been sold, however, resulting in the presence of several hundred private land owners in this region.

The rancher here leases grazing rights from BLM. This grazing lease consists of 450,000 acres. The lessee is permitted to graze 266 head. The actual number grazed depends upon the condition of grass. In dry years -- such as the case over the past few years -- range conditions are poor and the rancher does not keep the maximum number of cattle on the range.

In the high country of the Old Woman Mountain there is a population of big horn sheep, possibly as many as sixty to eighty. These will occasionally be seen by travelers on the Heritage Trail.

There is a controversy about whether or not cattle and big horn sheep can live in close proximity, as they do in this region, without the sheep suffering from the presence of cattle. While you will hear highly emotional and definitive statements on both sides of the issue from time to time, the scientific data available does not show any adverse effects. Range cattle have been existing side-by-side with big horn sheep in the East Mojave for more than 100 years and the sheep are faring better now than

Sunflower Springs
Most of the buildings were constructed
by Jim Craig.
The area around Sunflower Springs
has now been fenced and you
must park outside.

This area is an important part of
Milton Blair's Lazy Daisy Ranch.
Be particularly careful not to disturb his
cattle or his property.

25 November 1989
Dennis Casebier Photo

TED JENSEN

Be sensitive to cattle ranching and to
the cattle themselves! Don't "push" cattle
if they are in the road -- give them the
right-of-way.

90.

they were when the white man first came, partly because they were hunted by Indians.

There is another controversy regarding competition between cattle and desert critters that comes to the front in this area. The desert tortoise has been listed by the State of California as a threatened species. There is fairly conclusive data to show that numbers of desert tortoises have decreased in recent decades, especially in the Western Mojave Desert. At the same time, while numbers of tortoises in the East Mojave may have decreased some, the decrease is not nearly as dramatic as in the Western Mojave. The tortoise having been listed as threatened causes every level of government to tighten up controls of all kinds in the areas considered to be desert tortoise habitat. So, while disease and drought are likely main reasons for decreases in tortoise numbers, cattle are also mentioned as somehow being a threat to the tortoise, so that controversy is raging in the California Desert also and it affects this area.

Meanwhile, despite all the controversy swirling around him, Rancher Milton Blair continues to raise cattle here and put beef on the tables of Americans.

Tred gently on this land where emotions are high. Take great care not to negatively impact the big horn sheep or desert tortoise and, at the same time, take great care not to negatively impact this great American cattle ranch. It represents an institution that has its roots at the very beginning of history in the American West. It is a way of life that is probably more threatened than either the big horn sheep or the desert tortoise.

45.2 *   **Continue ahead (northeast) through fence line. El. 3,280 ft. (0.2).**

45.4 *   **Continue ahead (east) crossing wash 20 feet wide. El. 3,230 ft. (0.7).**

46.1 *   **Continue ahead (southeast) past Sunflower Springs Road crossroad. Be alert for a narrow "Y" coming up in 0.3 miles. El. 3,050 ft. (0.3).**

46.1   THE OLD WOMAN METEORITE. One of the great thrills of visiting the East Mojave is observing the heavens on a clear night. The comments you'll hear on such an occasion include: "I didn't know there were so many stars" and "I haven't seen stars like this since I was a child." Then someone will notice a satellite passing overhead. Then suddenly a visitor from space may streak across the sky -- a shooting star or meteorite. Generally their passing will be so fast and cover so brief a time that maybe only one or two in a party will see it. Much rarer is observation of a larger meteorite, perhaps even one that may hit the ground.

There is not much mention of meteorites in old written records for the East Mojave. The following article is an exception. It appeared in the April 3, 1865 issue of a California newspaper under a dateline of "Fort Mojave, Arizona Territory, March 20, 1865.

"A loud noise, supposed to be the report of a meteor, was heard a few weeks ago about ten o'clock at night. It was distinctly heard for twenty miles up and

LUCKY JIM MINE

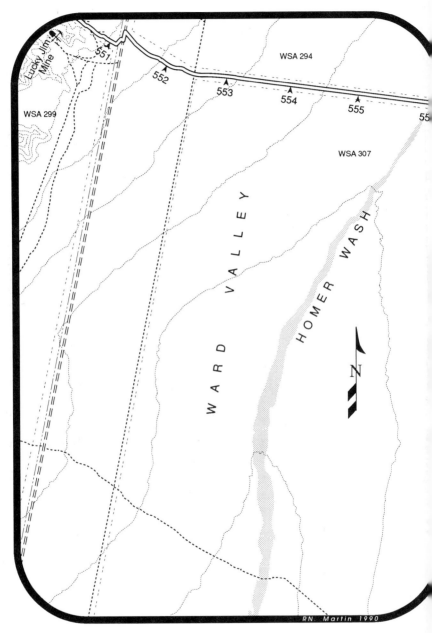

"HOW LUCKY CAN YOU GET... YOU JUST FOUND A METEORITE!"

95.

down the river, and also in the Irataba district the repor
was very heavy, and it is claimed that the place where i
struck has been found there. The rocks and earth are sai
to be rent and torn up fearfully. If it was a meteor, i
might be profitable to mine there for aero-ites." Mentio
of the "Irataba district" would place the point of impac
somewhere to the southwest of Fort Mojave.

One time many years ago a huge meteorite lande
in the Old Woman Mountains. It was discovered in 197
and instantly became the focus of controversy about wh
owned it. Geologist Steve Pencall has written an accoun
of what has become known as *The Old Woman Meteorite*
It is reproduced in the Appendix on pages 271 throug
272.

546.4 *   *   "Y." Bear right (south) at this narrow sand
**"Y." Trail is very sandy and frequently carries wate
drainage. El. 2,990 ft. (2.0).**

548.4 *   **Continue ahead (southeast). Ignore road righ
up wash. El. 2,490 ft. (1.8).**

550.2 *   **Ignore road to Oro Plata Mine on right 200 fee
in Old Woman Mountains. El. 2,170 ft. (0.2).**

550.2   Oro Plata (means gold-silver in Spanish). Minera
in quartz veins include galena (lead sulfide) whic
contains silver. Copper minerals present inclu
chrysocolla (blue green) and chalcopyrite (brassy). Gol
if present, is free in quartz veins. The veins were form
as the outer solid shell of the granodiorite intrusi
cracked and permitted hot fluid containing the minerals
escape from the still molten center. This is called

"hydrothermal ore deposit." SP.

0.4 *   *   **"Y." Bear left (southeast). El. 2,100 ft. (0.3).**

0.7 *   *   **"Y." Bear left (straight -- southeast). El. 2,040 ft. (0.1).**

0.8 *   *   **"Y." Bear right (straight -- southeast). El. 2,000 ft. (0.3).**

1.0   Crossing the basin (valley) between the Old Woman Mountains and the Turtle Mountains, the Trail traverses the pediment, the bajada, (the playa lake is to the south), and then the pediment of the Turtles. This is a very nice sequence of the geomorphology of a desert basin or valley. JV.

1.1 *   **Continue ahead (east). Ignore road coming in from right rear. El. 1,950 ft. (0.1).**

1.2 *   *   **"Y." Bear left (northeast). El. 1,940 ft. (0.0+).**

1.2+   **   **Turn left (north) on wide graded power line road. El. 1,940 ft. (0.1).**

1.2+   This is a line utilized by the Metropolitan Water District to supply power for pumping water along the Colorado River Aqueduct that conveys water from Lake Havasu behind Parker Dam to the Los Angeles area. (The immediate destination of that water is the holding reservoir at Lake Matthews near Riverside.) This 220 KV line carries electrical power from Hoover Dam to the pumping stations at Iron Mountain and other points.

"Are you in there?" the burro seems to be asking.
There are abandoned mines and prospects galore
in the California Desert. Some are large and some are
small, and most of them are dangerous.
Be extremely careful when in the vicinity of
old mines. Be especially careful to keep track
of children and pets. It is best just to steer
away from them.

October 1927
Susie Keef (Smith) Fry Collection

98.

Construction of this line commenced in December of 1935 and it was placed in service in 1939. The power transmitted in this line is alternating current and hence it requires three wires for one circuit. The contractor's main camp was at Camino to the north of here at the intersection of this power line and I-40 (then U.S. Highway 66).

1.2+ LUCKY JIM MINE. The Lucky Jim Mine is situated in a canyon just to the south of here. It is private property and should not be visited without permission of the owner. Also, as an additional inducement to stay away, it features a long horizontal entry tunnel that is extremely dangerous. So it is a good place to stay away from on several counts. In many ways its history is much like that of other desert mines. It has been a promising silver deposit and it has been worked several times between the time of its discovery in 1911 and 1930. A distinctive thing about the Lucky Jim Mine is that I had the good fortune to make the acquaintance of a man who was a "hard rock miner" in the Lucky Jim in the late '20s and early '30s. And, fortunately for us, Thomas W. Cooper was also a writer. In later years he wrote a series of essays about hard rock mining in the East Mojave. He called these essays "episodes." One of his "episodes" has been reproduced in the Appendix on pages 273 through 290.

1.2+ CADIZ (OR PARKER) CUTOFF OF THE A.T.&S.F.R.R. A branch to Phoenix leaves the main line of the Santa Fe at Cadiz and heads southeast towards a crossing of the Colorado River at Parker. This branch crosses Ward Valley about fifteen miles to the south of

this point. It is important to this area when the mines a
active providing convenient sidings at places li
Chubbuck and Milligan. It was very important to t
Desert Training Center during World War II as ma
troops and supplies were unloaded at Freda and Rice.

551.3 * ***** **Turn right (southeast) off power line road**
head east across wide Ward Valley toward the no
end of the Turtle Mountains for the next 9.6 miles.
1,940 ft. (1.2).

552.5 * ***** **Cross gas line road, and join Parker 400 ra**
course (which comes in from the right) genera
heading east for the next 8.4 miles. El. 1,720 ft. (3.

552.5

THERE IS HERITAGE EVERYWHERE
ALONG THE
EAST MOJAVE HERITAGE TRAIL

There are symbols of our history at every turn
the Heritage Trail. Recently, when we were along
Heritage Trail in Ward Valley, Jo Ann Smith said "wh
that?" and started to bend to pick something up. Then
instinctively pulled back knowing we'd want
photograph it *in situ*. It was a set of dog tags of Wo
War II vintage -- complete with chain. How long had t
been there? What happened to the owner? What st
could this symbol of the past tell?

The dog tags gave the man's name, Robert
Colbert, his army serial number, his blood type, the na
of his next of kin, and his religious affiliation.

About a week later I decided to see if I could f
the answers. The name of next of kin included an addre
It was obviously the man's mother and the address wa

small town in Indiana. Knowing there was a good chance his mother was deceased, still, in a small town, there was a chance I could get the answers over the phone so I decided to call.

To make a long story short, with about five long-distance phone calls and a half hour later, I had Robert H. Colbert himself on the phone in Florida. He had been at the Desert Training Center in 1942. He wasn't sure where he was -- that's fairly common for the DTC was very spread out and units were moved around. He remembered Rice and Needles. He was with the 5th Armored Division; they thought they were going to North Africa. But by the time they completed their training, Rommell had been driven from North Africa. After some delay they were sent to England. They landed at Normandy at D + 5. They campaigned clear across Europe to Czechoslovakia. Robert came back.

Of course he was surprised to hear this voice from the past asking him "Private Colbert, can't you keep track of your dog tags?" For 48 years those dog tags had laid out there. And they were no worse for the wear. They are in near mint condition.

There is history everywhere in the East Mojave. Sometimes you find it in concrete slabs that mark the site of some forgotten dream. Sometimes it is in the form of initials chiseled into sandstone. Sometimes it is wheel ruts in rock or hard soil. And sometimes it is dog tags lost on the road to Normandy!   Thanks, Robert, thanks for Normandy and thanks for losing your dog tags.

5.0 *   **Cross Homer Wash 100 feet wide and start up slight grade. Trail changes color from sandy to grey. Smoke trees in wash. El. 1,360 ft. (1.4).**

HOMER WASH

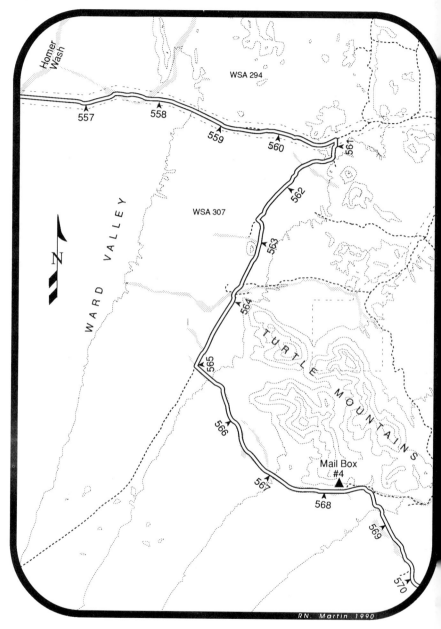

5.0   The color change in the sand of the Trail is due to the weathering of volcanic rocks in the Turtle Mountains in contrast to the Old Woman Mountains which contain practically no volcanic rocks. The Turtle Mountains ahead are a complex region where a varied mixture of volcanic rocks 18-22 million years old (Miocene) overlies an assemblage of igneous and metamorphic rocks up to 1.5 billion years old (Precambrian). The range is broken into numerous blocks by a series of northwest-trending faults. Geologic evidence suggests that the blocks became progressively detached from the Whipple Mountains to the east, slid away from the Whipple Mountains on a detachment fault, removing support from an adjoining mass of rock, which in turn broke along a line of weakness and began to slide. An apt analogy is calving of icebergs by a glacier. SP.

7.4 *   **Cross wash 200 feet wide at an angle. Smoke trees in wash. El. 1,420 ft. (0.5).**

7.9 *   **Cross wash 100 feet wide with smoke trees. El. 1,440 ft. (1.3).**

7.9   The rambling milkweed can be seen climbing over the shrubs in the wash at this point on the Trail.

9.2 * *   **Narrow "Y." Bear right (straight east). El. 1,510 ft. (0.2).**

9.4 *   **Pass dark butte 150 feet high on left 0.1 mile. El. 1,520 ft. (0.9).**

9.3 * *   **"Y." Bear left (east). Road splits at a narrow**

Indians made use of every nook and cranny of the desert.
Almost everywhere you can find traces of their passing.
In many places the signs of different Indian civilizations
are intermixed. There are petroglyphs, pictographs,
intaglios, sleeping circles, kitchen middens, and
many other signs.
The "sleeping circles" in this picture mark
an early Indian campsite.

We do not pinpoint archeological sites. If you are
patient and observant, you will run across them.
Enjoy them, photograph them, but leave them
as you find them. If you think you have
located an unknown site, report its location
to the Bureau of Land Management in Needles.
Wilma (Buechen) Krause Collection

angle. Trail (left road) is most heavily traveled. You are entering north end of Turtle Mountains. El. 1,580 ft. (0.2).

0.3   To the north of the Trail clumps of the rush milkweed can be observed. Desert lavender, creosote bush, burro bush, sweetbush, catclaw acacia, odora, hedgehog cactus, barrel cactus, pencil cholla, golden/silver cholla, inflated buckwheat, rattlesnake weed, and fluff grass may also be observed in this area.

0.5 *   **Ignore road rejoining from right rear. El. 1,580 ft. (0.4).**

0.5   Butte on left (north) is welded tuff with a set of regular joints that cause the rock to weather to rounded boulders much like granite. SP.

CAUTION!
At Mile 560.9 the Trail enters an inaccessible, isolated, and difficult section of the EAST MOJAVE HERITAGE TRAIL. Several vehicles have experienced tire problems at Mile 571.9+. Under no conditions should single vehicles traverse this section of the Trail.
CAUTION!

50.9 *   *   **Turn right (south) off main road. Trail ahead is visible on hill 0.2 miles south looking toward butte with split ("V") in it 0.4 miles away. The "V" is on the smaller butte to the right of the taller one. This is the point where a side trip can be made to the Lost Arch Inn. El. 1,600 ft. (0.3).**

105.

A caravan approaching "the notch" near Mile 560.9
in the Turtle Mountains.

25 November 1989
Dennis Casebier Photo

SIDE TRIP TO THE LOST ARCH INN

0.0   At Mile 560.9 continue straight (east) instead of turning right.

0.6   Small rocky knob 15 feet high on right 150 feet. Trail is very rough for next 1.8 miles from race use.

1.1   Old chimney 400 feet on left. This is also the crest of the route across the north end of the Turtle Mountains.

2.4   Turn right (southwest) off race course road. There is a mail box on a post at this junction.

3.4   Turn left (southeast). On the right is a cleared area where a shack formerly stood.

4.7   Continue ahead (south). Ignore road right.

4.8   Cross sand wash 100 feet wide and continue southeast.

4.9   Continue ahead (southeast). Ignore roads left and right.

4.9+   Continue ahead (southeast). Ignore road coming in from left rear.

5.3   Cross wash 10 feet deep and 200 feet wide.

5.5   Continue ahead (south). Ignore road left.

5.6   Continue ahead (south) past collapsed shack on right. Ignore roads left and right.

5.7   "Y." Bear left (south).

5.9   Cross wash 20 feet deep and 100 feet wide.

6.2   Continue ahead (south). Ignore road left.

6.4   Continue ahead (south). Ignore road left.

6.5   Continue ahead (south). Ignore road coming in from right rear.

7.5   Mill site foundations left 0.1 mile.

7.7   Lost Arch Inn. To continue on the Trail, return by the route you just took to Mile 560.9 and turn left (south).

Until very recent times the Turtle Mountains have been an isolated and little-known corner of the desert. Even so, the area was penetrated by prospectors and other adventurers even before the beginning of this century. In common with most other desert areas, the Turtle Mountains have played host to a number of desert personalities ... "personalities" may not be the right word, "characters" may be closer. One of the most colorful inhabitants of the Turtle Mountains region was a man named Christopher "Kit" Carson who held forth in the north end of the mountains through the teens and into the twenties. Carson Spring in the Turtles is named for this colorful individual. "Kit," who claimed to be a grandson of the famous mountain man and guide, managed to obtain some color of title to many of the mines and prospects of this region. He managed to interest "capital" in some of his "properties" so there was a fair amount of traffic from Needles to this isolated spot throughout the years he was here.

Later another desert personality named Charley Brown lived in much the same area Kit Carson had occupied. There is an excellent article about the Turtle Mountains by the desert writer Mary Frances Strong in the February 1971 issue of *Desert Magazine* wherein she provides the following insight pertaining to Charley Brown and his cabin, which became known as the "Lost Arch Inn:"

"Continuing south, an old mill site will be seen; and, as the road curves east the Lost Arch Inn looms into view. The 'Inn,' which has appeared on many old road maps, is only a couple of wooden cabins. It was the home of Charley Brown, an old-time desert prospector, who came to the Turtles in 1922 and lived there until his death in 1948. Charley knew every nook and cranny of the Turtles, as well as their many gem fields. His interest was only in gold and silver and he worked a mine in the Turtles with his partner, Jesse Craik. How well I recall sitting around the campfire and listening spellbound to their stories about the Turtles. It was here I first heard of the deposit of chalcedony on Jesse Craik's perlite claim. 'Young lady, if you want roses, you will find thousands of them eroding out of the hillside. Help yourself,' Jesse advised me. I did and, as Jesse said -- there were thousands!"

END OF SIDE TRIP

561.2 *   *   "Y." Bear right (west) just after crest and [
west around southern side slope of hill. El. 1,640 f
(0.4).

561.6 *   *   Turn left (southwest) away from hill on rigl
and immediately cross sand wash 20 feet wide. Ignor
tracks and cross-trails as you proceed southwe
alongside Turtle Mountains one mile left. El. 1,590 f
(0.5).

562.1 *   Continue ahead (southwest). Cross wash 15 fe
deep. El. 1,590 ft. (0.4).

562.5 *   *   Turn left (south). El. 1,600 ft. (0.2).

562.7 *   Cross wash 30 feet wide and 10 feet deep an
continue southwest. El. 1,610 ft. (0.4).

563.1 *   Continue ahead (southwest). Dark isolated butt
500 feet high on right 100 yards. Ignore many cro:
trails. Rocky. El. 1,640 ft. (0.5).

563.1   Dark butte on right (west) 100 yards is a volcani
rock called andesite, here containing green crystals c
hornblende. SP.

563.6 *   *   Bear right (southwest), intersecting bette
traveled road. El. 1,610 ft. (0.2).

563.8 *   *   Continue ahead (southwest) across large was
200 feet wide. Ignore faint road right. Ignore road le
after crossing wash. El. 1,600 ft. (0.1).

63.9 *   **Point of mountain 0.1 mile on left. El. 1,590 ft. (0.7).**

64.6 *   **Cross two washes each 20 feet wide. El. 1,440 ft. (0.4).**

64.6   A shrub in the spurge family, the purple-bush (*Tetracoccus hallii*) can be seen in the washes that cut the Trail in this area. This shrub is dioecious, meaning that there are male and female plants. Close examination will show that a plant will have male (stamens only) or female (pistle only) flowers. This is one of only three species of *Tetracoccus* that occur in California. The generic name refers to the four parted *Tetra* fruit *coccus* that occur on the female plants in this genus.

Large green shrubs or small trees observed in washes on this side of the Turtle Mountains are the palo verde (*Cercidium floridum*). The chlorophyll in the bark of the stems allows this plant to drop its leaves during periods of water stress and still maintain some photosynthetic ability by using the stem tissues. When in bloom this plant is quite beautiful with its large bouquets of yellow flowers. These flowers are the favorite feeding grounds for many insect pollinators, especially bees. Vision for bees is in the ultra-violet wave lengths so they see shades of gray between white and black. The flowers of the palo verde are composed of five petals some of which fade after the flower is pollinated. This fading is not striking to us seeing in the color wave lengths, but to the bee seeing in UV, the faded petals are white and very obvious. The flower stops producing nectar after it is pollinated so after experiencing no reward the bee learns that flowers with the white petals are no good and thus

111.

The wind can blow with unbelievable intensity
in the desert.
Secure your camp before bedding down at night.

concentrates on the unpollinated flowers. This increases the reproductive output of the palo verde while saving the bees' energy so both partners in this interesting relationship gain. Closer observation shows that some of the palo verde in this area are infested with the California mistletoe so the phaenopepela (the black bird with a crest) will be seen in this area feeding on the mistletoe berries.

5.0 * ** **Turn left (southeast) just before large smoke tree wash. Major intersection marked by metal post. Trail wanders in and out of a wash and you are headed up wash. El. 1,610 ft. (1.4).

5.0   A portion of the Turtle Mountains is close at hand. Here is a good location to ponder the enormity of the molten material that poured out to create these mountains -- millions upon millions of tons of molten rock. JV.

6.4 * **Continue ahead up wash (southeast) bearing left just after large isolated palo verde tree on right 30 feet high. El. 1,740 ft. (1.1).**

7.5 * **Trail is alongside mountain immediately on your left and stays generally near the edge of mountain for the next mile. El. 1,850 ft. (0.5).**

7.5   Hill on left (north) has basalt exposed at base. SP.

7.9   Basalt on left contains calcite and quartz crystals filling the gas bubbles. SP.

8.0 * ** **"Y." Bear left (east). Wash splits. Continue hugging mountain on left. El. 1,890 ft. (0.1).

(above) *Friends of the Mojave Road*
pose for a photograph after installation
of the Mail Box on the Fourth Segment,
East Mojave Heritage Trail.

(right) Frank Tomlinson sets up camp
on the East Mojave Heritage Trail
near the Mail Box on the Fourth Segment.

Mile 568.1 -- 4 March 1990
Dennis Casebier Photos

114.

568.0   As you continue up the wash you will see smoke trees, desert lavender, cheese bush, palo verde, sandpaper plant, and thick-leaved ground cherry (*Physalis crassifolia crassifolia*).

568.1 *   *   MAIL BOX. The Mail Box for the Fourth Segment sits up out of the wash to the left. It was fabricated by Bill Bains, Dick MacPherson, and Rick MacPherson and installed by a group of the *Friends of the Mojave Road* on March 4, 1990. Please stop and sign in. Give us your comments about how the Trail might be better interpreted and any other ideas you'd like to share. El. 1,910 ft. (0.2).

68.2   Straight ahead is a very serrated range -- many pinnacles and colors blending into the volcanic material. To the right in the reddish volcanics is a cliffed mesa. A harder, resistant capping rock has made the mesa. The underlying rock materials are much weaker and more easily eroded thereby creating the cliffed effect. To the north, the change in rock color is an indication in change in rock characteristics: volcanic to metamorphic to granite. JV.

68.3 *   *   "Y." Bear right (south) away from mountains. El. 1,920 ft. (1.0).

69.3 *   *   "Y." Bear left (southeast) in wash. El. 1,920 ft. (0.1).

69.4 *   *   Bear right (south) in wash. Scenic valley on left with jagged peaks. El. 1,930 ft. (0.5).

69.9 *   Continue ahead up wash (southeast) toward gap in hills. Ignore road right which goes into a closed area. El. 2,030 ft. (0.9).

70.7   Basalt with chalcedony cavity fillings on right. Chalcedony is a very fine-grained form of quartz. SP.

70.8 *   Continue ahead (southeast). Ignore road entering from right rear which goes into a closed area. El. 2,220 ft. (0.1).

MOPAH PEAKS

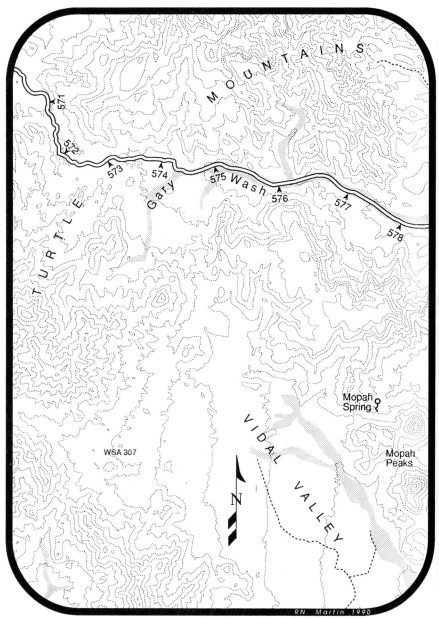

118.

0.9 *   Trail is close alongside mountain on your left. El. 2,230 ft. (0.7).

0.9   Fine-grained andesite on left which cooled in a shallow intrusion. SP.

1.1   Lineated granite on right. Lineation is a texture resulting from metamorphic pressure. We have entered the Precambrian core of the Turtle Mountains. SP.

1.3   Migmatite on left. Migmatite is a term describing a rock having a composite of textures and compositions of both igneous and metamorphic rocks. The migmatites here are believed to have formed from partial melting of rocks during metamorphism. They often display intricate folding. Migmatites will be exposed along the Trail for the next 1.8 miles. SP.

1.6 *   *   "Y." Bear right (south). Mountains on both sides. El. 2,340 ft. (0.1).

1.7 *   *   Five foot steel pole 10 feet on right. El. 2,360 ft. (0.2).

1.7   Unconformity on right. Fanglomerate overlying shattered migmatite. Fanglomerate is a conglomerate rock formed from the coarse angular gravel of alluvial fans. An unconformity is a surface that indicates a gap in the geologic record as here where a long period of erosion preceded deposition of the fanglomerate. SP.

1.9 *   *   "T." Take very narrow wash left (east) over ledge (up wash). This is the bad spot mentioned in the

CAUTION at Mile 560.9. There are about four on foot ledges a few hundred feet apart. Have faith Tracks may go right -- do not go right (dead end) as i is a closed area. El. 2,400 ft. (0.4).

571.9   In making the turn into the narrow canyon, on th left side is an excellent example of highly metamorphose rock called gneiss (characterized by the definite minera streaks). This type of metamorphic rock originally cam from granite and then was subjected to high-grad metamorphic action (long-term pressure and heating which caused a partial recrystallizing of certain mineral and the concentration of said minerals. The canyon is very good example of the activities associated with a fau line: movement along the fault caused a great fracturin of the rock, which, in turn, stream activity could remov -- thus creating a narrow water gap in hard, resistar rock. Granite outcrops make up the one foot ledges in th Trail in the canyon. JV.

572.3 *   Continue ahead (east) out of narrow part wash. El. 2,490 ft. (0.2).

572.3   Shrub in area where the Trail cuts through narro canyon indicating moisture is emory baccharis in th sunflower family as well as sweetbush, desert lavende catclaw acacia, goldeneye, California buckwheat, creoso bush, white ratney, Nevada Mormon tea, barrel cactu and arrowbush.

572.5 *   *   Cross watershed (crest) of Turtles, contint ahead, downhill, east, to soon (0.2 miles) enter Ga

121.

Wash and head down wash for the next 7.3 miles. El. 2,540 ft. (1.3).

572.5   Green Mormon tea occurs here at the higher elevations along with the grizzly cactus, and fishhook cactus (*Mammillaria tetrancistra*).

572.5   Pass area. Migmatite here is composed of bands several feet thick. You are traversing a topographic basin in the core of the Turtle Mountains uplift. SP.

573.2   Solidified volcanic mudflow to right overlain by basalt flow just downstream. SP.

573.4   Pink tuff on right with more resistant brown-weathering rock fragments etched out by erosion. SP.

573.8 *   **Pass point of rocks on left. Continue southeast down wash. El. 2,340 ft. (1.0).**

573.8   Three basalt flows on left stacked on top of one another. The flows are gray or brown and separated by reddish or purple clinker zones. The clinkers are fragments formed as the surfaces of the lava flow cool and break up as the flow continues moving. SP.

574.1   Greenish rock on left is a quartz gneiss with abundant biotite mica giving it a greenish hue. SP.

574.5   On both sides of the Trail vertical cliffs appear looking like organ pipes or columnar basalt. This is another example of differences in hardness of rock strata: cliffs and bluffs above representing the more resistant rock and the slopes representing softer material. JV.

4.8 *   **Continue ahead (southeast) down wash filled with smoke trees. El. 2,200 ft. (1.0).**

4.8   Gary Wash is an excellent example of a wash with enough periodic flooding that it supports a dense population of smoke trees. In this wash also will be seen palo verde, cheesebush, sandpaper plant, ocotillo, and creosote bush on the slopes at the lower elevations. Desert lavender, scented penstemon, coyote melon, golden/silver cholla, grizzly cactus, brittle bush, white ratney, wire lettuce, and large barrel cactus are very abundant before the Trail emerges from the wash.

4.8   Peak on left capped by welded dacite tuff unit 150 feet thick. SP.

5.0   Red rock on left is a 6 - 8 feet layer of sandstone composed largely of red sand-sized volcanic fragments overlying a welded latite tuff. The fragments easily weather free and veneer the slope, making the layer appear thicker than it actually is. SP.

5.3   Wash entering from right drains an area of volcanic rocks and its darker sand and gravel markedly contrasts with the lighter sand of Gary Wash. SP.

5.4   Cemented basalt scoria (volcanic cinders) on right. SP.

5.5   The brighter rock strata to the right represent a magmatic intrusion into already existing volcanic rock: the horizontal section would be called a sill (a tabular intrusion that is generally parallel to the surrounding country rock). The vertical segment to the left end of the intrusion would be a dike (a tabular intrusion that is generally not parallel or concordant to the invaded country rock). JV.

575.6   Volcanic mudflow on right. Volcanism produces much loose debris from dust-sized to boulder-sized which forms a thick mud-like wet concrete when saturated. These mudflows are capable of traveling a great distance from their source. SP.

575.7   Welded tuffs form the prominent cliffs up the canyon to the left. Such landscapes are reminiscent of the Colorado Plateau of Utah and Arizona although the rock types are completely different. Although they cannot be easily seen from the Trail, numerous steeply dipping faults (normal faults) cut this portion of the Turtle Mountains so that a cross-section view would resemble a row of toppled dominoes in the position in which they fell. SP.

575.8 *   **Trail is on the right hand side of wash. El. 2,080 ft. (1.0).**

576.0   Reddish welded tuffs to left and right. SP.

576.7   Ridgeline on right has a sinuous volcanic dike climbing up it at a steep angle at about 1:30 to a point slightly more than one-third of the way up the ridge. Dike is just to the left and above the pinnacle in foreground. Several other dikes may be observed in the area. Dikes are formed as the earth's crust is stretched, allowing fractures to form along zones of weakness. Molten lava is

GARY WASH

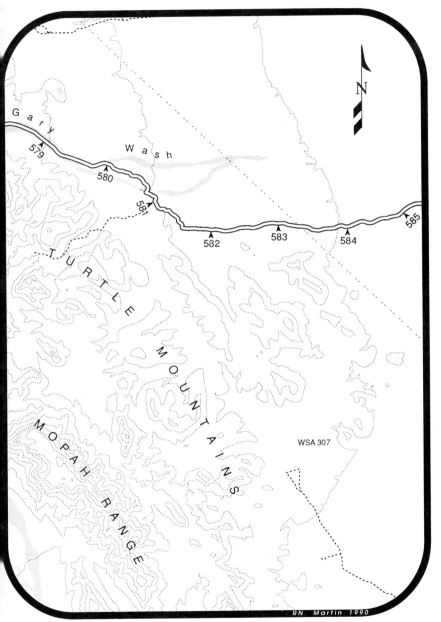

N

G a r y

W a s h

579
580
581
582
583
584
585

TURTLE MOUNTAINS

MOPAH RANGE

WSA 307

RN. Martin 1990

then injected into the fracture under fluid pressure. SP.

576.8 *   **Continue ahead (southeast) down wash witl many smoke trees. El. 1,980 ft. (1.8).**

578.6 *   **Continue ahead (southeast) down smoke tre wash. Mopah Peaks visible on right three miles (thes are the two tall isolated steep-sided peaks). El. 1,78 ft. (1.4).**

580.0 * *   **Trail turns right (south) out of wash. El. 1,68 ft. (0.8).**

580.0   Growing up through the desert pavement can b seen solitary barrel cactus and occasional pencil cholla. /
close look at the desert pavement will show many annua plants in the spring. The dead remnants of one of thes from previous years with its spiny bracts and reddis color is the spiny desert-herb.

580.4   Good view: Chemehuevi Mountains at 11:30 wit the lower Sawtooth Range in front, Whipple Mountain ahead at 12:30. The Mopah Peaks at 3:00 are rhyolit volcanic necks. The necks formed as pasty rhyolite fille volcanic vents and later erosion stripped away the softe surrounding rocks leaving necks to stand out in relief. SP

580.8 *   **Continue ahead (southeast) after crossin; arroyo 15 feet deep and 30 feet wide. El. 1,610 ft (0.2).**

581.0 * *   **Continue ahead (southeast). Ignore road righ to Mopah Springs. (You can visit Mopah Springs b;**

PYRAMID BUTTE

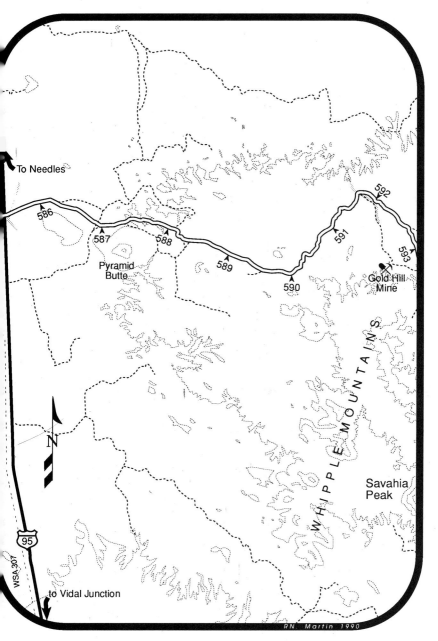

To Needles

586
587
588
589
590
591
592
593

Pyramid
Butte

Gold Hill
Mine

N

95

WSA-307

to Vidal Junction

W H I P P L E   M O U N T A I N S

Savahia
Peak

R.N. Martin 1990

taking the road to the right, following it to the end and hiking three miles up the wash.) El. 1,600 ft (0.4).

581.4 *   Jog left across sand wash. El. 1,580 ft. (2.2).

583.6 *   Continue ahead (southeast). Ignore roa entering from right rear. El. 1,430 ft. (1.8).

585.4 *   *   Reach U.S. Highway 95. Continue ahea straight (east) across highway. El. 1,320 ft. (0.1).

CAUTION!
THERE IS HIGH SPEED TRAFFIC ON THIS
HIGHWAY THAT IS NOT EXPECTING
SLOW CROSS TRAFFIC.
CAUTION!

585.4   To the south on this highway it is a little over 1 miles to Vidal Junction on California State Highway 6 that runs between 29 Palms, California, and Parke Arizona on the Colorado River. From Vidal Junction it less than 20 miles to Parker. Parker is headquarters fc the Colorado River Indian Reservation that occupies mor than a quarter of a million acres in the river valley sout of Parker. This reservation was established in 1865 fc Hualapai, Yavapai, and Colorado River Tribes. Th included the Chemehuevi Indians, many of whom ha formerly occupied the East Mojave Desert. It was als designed to include the Mojave Indians. About half th tribe settled on that reservation and the other ha remained on their ancestral lands in the Colorado Rive Valley between the modern Needles on the south an

Laughlin and Bullhead City on the north. The name Parker was originally used in this area in honor of Gen. Eli Parker who was commissioner of Indian Affairs in the early 1870s. It happens that the locating engineer for the A.T.& S.F.R.R. Company when they laid their line through Parker in the early 1900s was Earl H. Parker, so it might be a question as to the origin of the name. Parker Dam took its name from the town.

It is about 95 miles from Vidal Junction to the west on Highway 62 to 29 Palms. To the north (that is if you turned left here) it is about 35 miles to Needles.

5.5 * **Continue ahead (east). Cross wash with heavy growth of creosote bushes and other plants. Ignore many faint cross tracks in area. El. 1,310 ft. (0.5).**

5.0 * **Continue ahead (east). Trail is faint. Black rounded butte on right 0.1 mile. El. 1,330 ft. (0.1).**

5.1 * * **Turn half right (southeast) on faint track pointing toward right edge of pyramid-shaped Pyramid Butte. El. 1,330 ft. (0.5).**

5.1 Large clumps of beavertail cactus in this area of the Trail as well as remnants of the spiny desert-herb. Creosote bush and burro bush are the dominant species with golden/silver cholla and pencil cholla contributing to the cacti of the area.

5.1 Butte on right and other dark buttes in area, including Pyramid Butte are the eroded remnants of basaltic cinder cones. SP.

Take Turns Driving.
It'll add to the enjoyment of the whole group.

5.6 *   *   "Y." Bear left (east) toward left side of Pyramid Butte. El. 1,340 ft. (0.0+).

5.6+   **   "Y." Bear left (straight) (east) toward left side of Pyramid Butte. El. 1,340 ft. (0.3).

5.6+   Odora, the pungent smelling plant in the sunflower family, is locally abundant.

5.9 *   *   Intersect major well traveled road and go left (southeast). El. 1,360 ft. (0.3).

7.2 *   *   "Y." Bear left (east). Major road goes both ways. In general, after bearing left, follow the main road the next 7.5 miles. El. 1,380 ft. (0.9).

8.0   Traveling through a landscape of multi-hued volcanic rocks, mostly rhyolite. There are many gold mines and prospects in the area. Gold is often associated with quartz and rhyolite is the most quartz-rich volcanic rock. SP.

8.1 *   *   "Y." Bear right, straight (southeast). El. 1,420 ft. (0.2).

8.3 *   *   "Y." Bear left (southeast). El. 1,440 ft. (0.1).

8.3   Teddy bear cholla appears on the slopes and flats along with buckhorn cholla and barrel cacti.

8.4 *   Continue ahead (east). Ignore road entering from right rear. El. 1,440 ft. (1.0).

WHIPPLE MOUNTAINS

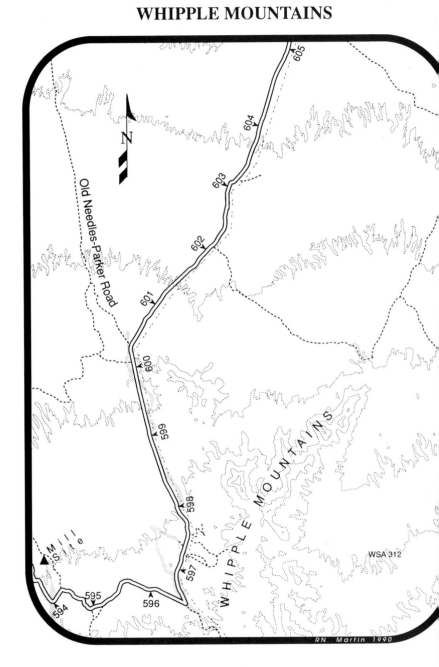

Old Mines are Dangerous.
STAY AWAY!

133.

589.4 * Cross small wash. Rocky butte on left 0.2 mile. Small rounded hill on right 0.1 mile. El. 1,480 f (0.3).

589.7 * Continue ahead (east). Ignore road enterin from right rear. El. 1,500 ft. (0.3).

590.0 * * Trail goes over small ridge and heads northea for one mile plus then loops back southeast. El. 1,52 ft. (0.6).

590.3 Greenish-gray rock on right is a small mass andesite that cooled in a very shallow intrustion. SP.

590.6 * Continue ahead (northeast). Cross large was 30 feet wide. El. 1,450 ft. (0.7).

591.3 * Trail turns east again. El. 1,440 ft. (0.6).

591.9 * Trail turns south. El. 1,440 ft. (0.8).

592.7 * * Continue ahead (southeast). Ignore road ar cairn on left. El. 1,520 ft. (0.7).

593.4 * Gold Hill Mill site visible left 0.2 miles. I 1,630 ft. (0.1).

593.5 * * "Y." Bear left (east). Road right leads to Go Hill Mine in 0.2 miles. El. 1,640 ft. (0.2).

593.5 In the Gold Hill Mine gold occurs in quartz ar calcite veins associated with diorite dikes that ha intruded schist. Considerable copper mineralization is al

Don't forget to "smell the roses."
Be sure to slow down and look at the desert
at your feet.

present. The principal period of mining activity was 190
1906. SP.

593.7 *   **Three foot square cairn on right 15 feet. I
1,600 ft. (0.1).**

593.7   Boxthorn and its relative peachthorn occur in th
area.

593.8 *   **Several shafts and prospects near road. I
1,660 ft. (0.2).**

594.0 *   **Cross wash 20 feet wide. Continue ahe
(northeast). El. 1,680 ft. (0.1).**

594.1 *   **Enter wash headed downhill (northeast) for
short distance. El. 1,680 ft. (0.1).**

594.2 *   *   **Turn right (southeast) out of wash. Ignore ro
left. (The Gold Hill mill site is 0.4 miles straight do
wash/road.) El. 1,660 ft. (0.5).**

594.7 *   *   **Turn left (east) leaving main road. Cairn. I
1,720 ft. (0.2).**

594.9 *   *   **Enter wash, immediately bear left and cr
wash 100 feet wide at 45° angle. El. 1,700 ft. (0.1).**

595.0 *   *   **Intersect major road. Bear left (northeast). I
1,690 ft. (0.4).**

595.4 *   **Cross wash 40 feet wide and continue northea
El. 1,680 ft. (0.4).**

5.5   Before entering wash there are barrel cactus, catclaw acacia, white ratney, turpentine-broom, fluff grass, creosote bush, burro bush, buckhorn cholla, teddy bear cholla, and indigo bush. In the wash the catclaw acacia has California mistletoe on it. Sweetbush, desert lavender, and the barrel cactus can be seen along the wash.

5.8 *   Cross wash 100 feet wide. Volcanic black spur is ahead half left 0.4 miles. El. 1,670 ft. (0.7).

6.5 * *   Turn hard left (northwest) almost 180⁰ to go downhill in sand wash. This is the old Needles-Parker Road. Ignore tracks up wash and also bulldozer road going up hill. Many whoop-dee-doos from Parker 400 race course use for the next 3.8 miles. El. 1,720 ft. (0.3).

6.8 * *   Trail exits wash right (north). You are now on a major ungraded road. El. 1,680 ft. (0.2).

7.0 *   Volcanic black spur left 100 yards. El. 1,690 ft. (0.3).

7.0   Hills on left and for next 0.5 miles are basalt scoria, or cinders, cemented by quartz and pockmarked by cavernous weathering. The amount of cement varies throughout the rock so that poorly cemented zones weather away more readily. We are skirting the western edge of the Whipple Mountains -- an area of intense geologic interest and research at present. The Whipple Mountains, like the Chemehuevi Mountains and Sacramento Mountains seen farther along the Trail have

137.

a complex history of crustal compression in the Mesozoi
Era (245 to 65 million years ago) followed by
geologically brief (about 12-15 million years) period c
crustal extension that began about 30 million years ago
This caused the phenomenon of detachment faulting. SF

597.0 These mountains are named for Amiel Week
Whipple who, as a first lieutenant in the Army Corps c
Topographical Engineers, led a government explorin
expedition through this country in 1854. His was one c
the expeditions that went out to determine the mo:
practical route for the Pacific Railroad. Whipple ha
instructions to follow the 35th Parallel of north latitude
He traveled from east to west. In western Arizona h
drifted south of the 35th Parallel because of scarcity c
water in the desert country between where Kingman i
now and the Colorado River. After striking the Colorad
River he went upstream to where Needles is now and the
continued his journey first northwest and then westwar
along the 35th Parallel to Cajon Pass and on into the Lo
Angeles basin. His large party included a military escor
scientists, artists. He gained the distinction to be the firs
person to take a wheeled vehicle through what we nov
call the East Mojave and over the Mojave Road. While
brigadier general of volunteers in the Union Army
Whipple died May 7, 1863 of wounds received at th
Battle of Chancellorsville on May 4, 1863. He had bee
promoted to the rank of major general of volunteers th
day before his death. His name has rightfully been place
in the heart of the desert country that he explored an
which was treated so fully and in accurate detail in hi
report.

Catclaw acacia is also known as the
"wait-a-minute" bush.

597.3 * Continue ahead (northeast). Fantastic hole mountains surround you. El. 1,640 ft. (1.1).

598.4 * Continue ahead (north). U.S.G.S. marker le 20 feet. Elevation 1,537 ft. (1.9).

598.5 At about 9:00 the Mopah Peaks (bypassed at Mi 578.6) are nicely visible. The peak is really a volcan plug of considerable height. The sister peak to the rigl (the flatter of the two peaks) has a very resistant layer c capping rock. JV.

598.9 Buckhorn cholla becomes very prevalent.

599.8 Large rectangular impressions in desert pavemer on right should be visible for a number of years. The were made in June 1989 by Vibroseis trucks doing seismi reflection work for the CALCRUST Program. Th program is operated by a consortium of souther California universities on a grant from the Nationა Science Foundation. The program was created in a attempt to determine the three-dimensional structure of th Earth's crust in California, information useful i exploration for petroleum and other resources, earthquak studies, and basic research.

The impressions were formed by large truck equipped with hydraulically actuated steel pads that thum the ground, creating waves that travel through the earth - like a small man-made earthquake. Some of the waves ar reflected when they reach a different type of rock and th reflected waves are monitored by sensors placed som distance away. Computers use the delay in arrival time o waves reflected from various layers to construct a profil of the deep crustal structure along the line from the trucks to the sensors.

The Whipple Mountains and surrounding areas have long been a candidate for studies of this kind because the surface geology is very complex and several models of the subsurface structure have been proposed to account for this. Many geologists believe that seismic reflection studies will help unravel this structural puzzle. SP.

.3 *   *   **"Y." Bear right (northeast) around point of mountain toward West Well leaving Parker 400 race course behind. Major intersection. Main Needles-Parker road went straight unless water was needed, then they went right to West Well. El. 1,320 ft. (0.1).**

.4 *   **Trail is on well defined road headed northeast. U.S.G.S. marker on left 10 feet. El. 1,310 ft. (0.8).**

.2 *   **U.S.G.S. marker on right 15 feet. El. 1,230 ft. (1.0).**

.2 *   **Continue ahead (northeast). Ignore road right. Note eight inch stub of old Department of the Interior signpost eight feet on right. El. 1,120 ft. (1.0).**

.2 *   **Continue ahead (northeast). Ignore road right. U.S.G.S. marker on right 20 feet. Trail drops into wash shortly. El. 1,060 ft. (2.9).**

.2   Just before dropping into the wash, straight ahead in the distance The Needles can be seen (for which the city of Needles is named). The Needles lie on the east

141.

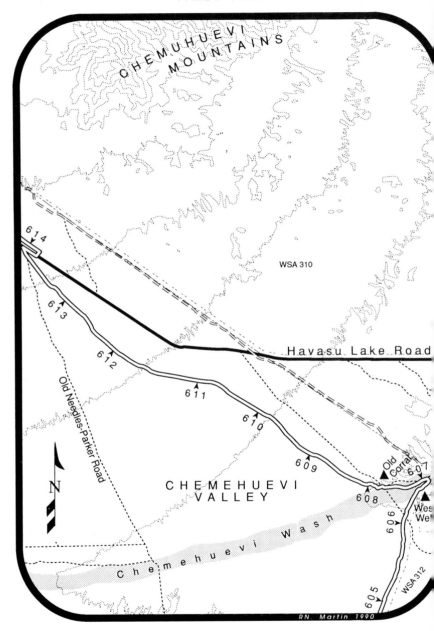

CHEMUHUEVI MOUNTAINS

614

613

612

611

610

609

WSA 310

Havasu Lake Road

Old Needles-Parker Road

N

CHEMEHUEVI VALLEY

Chemehuevi Wash

Old Corral

607

608

606

West Well

605

WSA 312

RN. Martin 1990

142.

side of the Colorado River between the city of Needles, California, and Havasu, Arizona. JV.

4.4   An excellent panoramic view of a typical desert landscape: at about 9:00, a fault-block mountain can be seen; clockwise at about 10:00, inselbergs drowning in the rock alluvial material; below the low foothills (the inselbergs) is the Chemehuevi Wash most of which is a bajada; at about 11:00, a line of volcanic peaks -- a series of domes nicely illustrated by the two lower ones in the center of the line; in the background of the volcanic landforms the whitish areas are playas; further in the background of the playa lakes are some massive fault-block mountains; at about 1:00, stretches the upper portions of a bajada -- actually the pediment -- extending into the base of the mountains at about 2:00 and 3:00. JV.

6.1 *   *   **Continue ahead (northeast). Ignore lesser road left and road right cut into hill. El. 810 ft. (0.4).**

6.1   Palo verde in wash and ocotillo on the flats. The wash also has a good population of odora so if you haven't stopped to smell that pungent odor, now is your chance. Smoke tree, catclaw acacia, cheesebush, sweetbush, and creosote bush can also be observed in the wash.

6.5 *   *   **West Well is the low covered four feet square structure alongside the northwest side of the modern corral on the south bank of Chemehuevi Wash and usually has water in it. Please do not pollute. Continue northeast to a fenced petroglyph site. El. 770 ft. (0.2).**

It is more difficult to get a good shot
of wildlife with a camera than with a gun,
and you and the wildlife will feel better too.

06.5   In the moist areas around the well and corral the arrow-weed can be seen.

06.5   West Well was on an early alignment of the old road that ran between Needles and Parker. The following description is from Walter C. Mendenhall's *Some Desert Watering Places* published in 1909: "This well is near the head of the Chemehuevi Wash, on the county road that runs from Needles, Cal., to Parker, Ariz. It is about 40 feet deep and stands in a clump of cottonwood trees. It is protected by curbing and provided with an iron pump and a good watering trough with cover. The water rises within about six feet of the surface and is of excellent quality. Since this well was dug the county road has been straightened. The main road now diverges from the old road about three miles west of this well and continues southward into the next township, where a new well has been dug. The old well is convenient for prospecting parties in the Chemehuevi Wash." The new well Mendenhall refers to was originally called "New West Well" and later it was called "Hanks Well." By 1917 Hanks Well was no longer functional so travelers needing water had to detour back on the old alignment to West Well. The following extract from David G. Thompson's book *The Mohave Desert Region California* published in 1929, but based largely on data gathered in 1917, describes this situation: "Formerly water could be obtained at Hanks Well, on the main road about midway between the two branch roads, but in November, 1917, the well was dry. Persons needing water could obtain it at West Well by making a detour of only about 3 1/2 miles. From West Well a road leads eastward down Chemehuevi Wash to Colorado River. Another road leads southward

145.

from West Well to Whipple Well and prospects in the Whipple Mountains." Many a traveler spreads his blankets in the soft sand of Chemehuevi Wash and in the protection, from wind or heat, of the large boulders that outcrop at West Well. And before them the Indians coveted this place, as indicated by the many petroglyphs on nearby boulders

TED JENSEN

06.7 *   *****   **Fenced petroglyph site on right 150 feet. Remain outside of fence. From petroglyph site, Trail continues northeast 200 feet then turns hard left (west) up 0.1 mile wide Chemehuevi Wash, soon moving to right (north) side of wash. This is the point from which a side trip to Havasu Lake (gas, services) can be made. El. 760 ft. (0.3).**

06.7   On right about 100 yards north of petroglyph site is a small bluff with interesting geological features. At the base is a pale greenish-yellow layer of water-laid tuff. Extending from the west (left) edge of the bluff is a bright pink band about 8 inches thick which abruptly ends about halfway across the bluff. The pink layer is a baked zone underlying a basalt flow. The bluff is capped by a volcanic mudflow composed largely of andesite fragments. The large pinkish boulders just north of the petroglyph site are dacite welded tuff. SP.

SIDE TRIP TO HAVASU LAKE

0.0   At Mile 606.7, continue east down Chemehuevi Wash.

0.1   Cross power line road and under power line.

1.3   Continue ahead (east) down wash leaving mountains behind.

3.8   Turn left (north) on pole line road and shortly

Flash floods can come up very quickly in
the desert, whether it is raining where
you are or not.
Don't camp in the washes!

148.

climb hill out of wash.

4.2   Turn right (east) on paved Havasu Lake Road.

5.2   Havasu Lake. Gas and cafe. To continue on the Trail, return by the route you just took to Mile 606.7 and go west up Chemehuevi Wash.

END OF SIDE TRIP

7.0 *   *   "Y." Bear right (west) in wash. El. 760 ft. (0.4).

7.4 *   *   Turn right (north) for 50 feet toward small, older corral on bank of Chemehuevi Wash. El. 790 ft. (0.0+).

7.4+   **   Turn left (southwest) 150 feet before reaching old corral. Ignore road continuing ahead (northwest) past corral fence & loading chute which is a mining road that follows the right (east) rim of a side wash northwest to Havasu Lake Road. A graded power line road also goes northwest to Havasu Lake Road and is a few tenths of a mile farther east. El. 790 ft. (0.1).

7.5 *   *   Turn right (north) up a side wash of Chemehuevi Wash for 0.2 miles. Stay on left side. This is a wash 200 feet wide after getting past entrance. El. 800 ft. (0.2).

7.7 *   *   Trail exits left bank of side wash to go northwest on the old Needles-Parker Road which follows top of west (left) rim of this side wash. Some creosote bushes are in the center of well defined wheel ruts. Straddle them, don't make new tracks. Mostly smooth road at first, washy areas will be rougher. Trail follows this road 6.3 miles to paved Havasu Lake Road. El. 810 ft. (1.6).

609.3 *   Trail bends a little left (northwest). El. 990 ft. (0.5).

609.8 *   U.S.G.S. marker on left 10 feet, elevation 1,048 feet. El. 1,050 ft. (0.5).

610.3 *   Trail heads west for a short distance. El. 1,100 ft. (0.9).

611.2 *   Continue ahead (west). Ignore several faint tracks left and right. El. 1,180 ft. (0.1).

611.3 *   Trail bends right a little toward northwest. El. 1,200 ft. (1.4).

611.3   Many ocotillo in this area.

612.7 *   Crossgrain/wash area. Trail is fainter here. Two barrel cacti close on left. El. 1,340 ft. (1.2).

613.9 *   *   Intersect and join old Needles-Parker Road coming in from left rear and continue northwest. Short eight inch remnants of old Department of the Interior post can be seen on the right of Trail five feet. El. 1,470 ft. (0.1).

614.0 *   *   Pavement (Havasu Lake Road). Turn right (southeast). The old road used to continue across but

SNAGGLE TOOTH

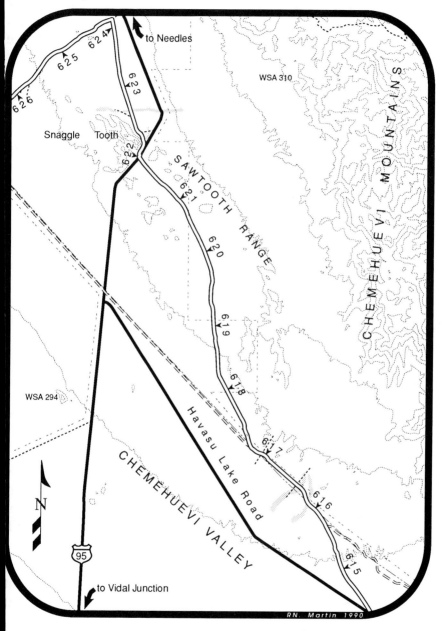

151.

a jog right (southeast) on pavement 0.2 miles is now necessary because of the berm on far side of pavement Turn left 180° (hairpin turn) at first break in berm on north side of road and go back (northwest) 0.2 mile in sand wash parallel and adjacent to pavement to where road would have crossed, and pick up old road by turning right (northwest). El. 1,480 ft. (0.4).

CAUTION!
THERE IS HIGH SPEED TRAFFIC ON THIS HIGHWAY THAT IS NOT EXPECTING SLOW CROSS TRAFFIC.
CAUTION!

614.4 *   *   Near pavement at Mile 614.0, headed northwest on the old road, after jog. El. 1,540 ft. (1.0).

614.4   Ocotillo, barrel cactus, buckhorn cholla, teddy bear cholla, beavertail cactus, creosote, burro bush, and white ratney on the flats and slopes, and catclaw acacia and cheesebush in the washes.

614.5   The southwest corner of the Chemehuevi Mountains is about 2 miles distant on the right (northeast). Like most other ranges in the region, the Chemehuevi Mountains have complex geology dominated by detachment faulting. They contain a lower plate consisting of a group of granitic intrusions of late Cretaceous age (about 65 million years old) which separated by a detachment fault from overlying gneisse and granitic rocks of Precambrian age (roughly 1.5 billion years old) and a complex group of Miocene age volcanic rocks (roughly 30 million years old). SP.

4.5　　　　　Chemehuevi Wash and Chemehuevi Mountains are named for the Chemehuevi Indians (an off-shoot of the Southern Paiute) who, when the white man first came to this country, occupied the great majority of the central part of the East Mojave, and much of the land now traversed by the East Mojave Heritage Trail. They were hunters and gatherers who were "one with the desert." Their food supply consisted of deer and mountain sheep, lizards, tortoises, jackrabbits and cottontails, and a great variety of edible seeds. They were spread thinly through their vast desert country. They moved around from place to place in response to the availability of game and the ripening of seeds. Because their land was so vast they had the option to melt into the vastness of their desert and carry on guerilla warfare with whites. They took that option with the result that the Indians of the desert were either exterminated or driven to reservations. They were a true desert people -- a wonderful people. Do yourself a favor and read the book *The Chemehievis* by the late Carobeth Laird and published by Malki Museum Press in 1976.

15.4 *　　　**Continue ahead (north). U.S.G.S. marker on left 15 feet. Many cholla and ocotillo. (Honk your horn and cholla joints will jump out of the tire tracks -- trust me.) [Editor's note: send all resulting tire repair bills to Neal Johns.] El. 1,610 ft. (0.4).**

15.8 *　*　**Turn left (north) on graded power line road as you intersect it. Trail will stay on power line road for 1.5 miles. El. 1,660 ft. (0.4).**

15.8　　　　　Greenish splotch on hill to right and on other hills in area is a diorite dike with abundant hornblende giving it the green color. Dikes form the prominent irregular dark lines on the slopes of the Chemehuevi and Sawtooth ranges visible for the next 3 miles. SP.

616.2 *   **Cross small sand wash 10 feet wide. Ignore any tracks in it. El. 1,690 ft. (0.0+).**

616.2+   *****   **Cross small sand wash 10 feet wide. Ignore any tracks in it. El. 1,690 ft. (0.3).**

616.5 *   **Continue ahead (northwest). Ignore road crossing. El. 1,720 ft. (0.5).**

617.0 *   **Continue ahead (northwest). Ignore road crossing. El. 1,700 ft. (0.1).**

617.1 *   **Continue ahead (northwest). Pass between low hills. El. 1,720 ft. (0.2).**

617.3 *   **Cross under power lines. El. 1,750 ft. (0.0+).**

617.3+   ******   **Exit power line road half-right (north) at shallow angle ahead on definite road, not a wash, crossing under power lines again. Ignore the several roads left and right off this old Needles-Parker Road as it goes 4.7 miles to U.S. Highway 95. El. 1,750 ft. (0.8).**

617.3+   Mojave yucca, indigo bush, wire lettuce, desert lavender, creosote bush, ocotillo, boxthorn, burro bush, California buckwheat, odora, brittle bush, buckhorn cholla, teddy bear cholla, barrel cactus, beavertail cactus on the slopes and flats and catclaw acacia, sweetbush, and cheesebush in the drainages.

7.4   Light-colored knoll on right 20 yards composed of quartz diorite is typical of rocks of the lower plate of the Chemehuevi Mountains. SP.

18.1 *   **Continue ahead (north) passing through low hills. El. 1,770 ft. (0.2).**

18.3 *   **Old Department of the Interior six foot post on right five feet. The Sawtooth Mountains are on the right 0.5 miles. El. 1,780 ft. (1.6).**

18.3   Bladder sage starts to occur in the drainages.

19.3   Now traveling through multi-hued terrain underlain by dacite lava that cooled in shallow intrusions. We have crossed the detachment fault and are now in the upper plate of the Chemehuevi Mountains. The linear trend of the volcanic northwest portion of the Sawtooth Mountains suggests that the volcanic vents which formed them were aligned along a fault. It is improbable, however, that the range was formed in a single eruption. Rather the eruptions are likely to have taken place over a period of millions of years as is the typical pattern of Mojave Desert volcanism. SP.

19.9 *   **Continue ahead (north) on long straight road. El. 1,880 ft. (1.7).**

21.6 *   **Sawtooth Range on the right (the Snaggle Tooth is across Highway 95 0.5 miles ahead). El. 1,900 ft. (0.4).**

Hiking in the desert can be rewarding.

1.6   Rush milkweed in this area of the Sawtooth Range.

2.0 *   *   Intersect U.S. Highway 95. Jog right 150 feet (northeast) on pavement and turn left off pavement. Trail heads north toward graffiti covered rocks at point of mountain. El. 1,890 ft. (0.1).

CAUTION!
THERE IS HIGH SPEED TRAFFIC ON THIS HIGHWAY THAT IS NOT EXPECTING SLOW CROSS TRAFFIC.
CAUTION!

22.1 *   Trail goes north up a wash. Graffiti covered rock is 100 feet left. U.S. Highway 95 is 50 feet right. El. 1,900 ft. (0.1).

22.2 *   *   Bear left (northwest) out of wash toward gap in hills (not pink bulldozer scrape visible on left). El. 1,910 ft. (0.1).

22.2   Snaggle Tooth on left is composed of (under graffiti) pink intrusive dacite porphyry. Porphyry is a texture of igneous rocks in which relatively large crystals (feldspar, in this case) occur in a fine-grained groundmass. SP.

22.2   Good solid historical facts for this region are scarce. On February 25 1938, when writing about the life of the late William Hutt, Needles pioneer Charles Battye included the following, thereby providing us with the source for the name Snaggle Tooth and some background on the Needles-Parker Road. "He laid out and built the first road to Parker, Arizona, and he gave the name Snaggletooth to that rough mountain twelve or fifteen miles south of Needles." In the early years of automobile travel, the Snaggletooth area served as a picnic spot for Needles people, who didn't have many places to go. The Needles papers frequently carried articles like the following: "PARTY TO SNAGGLETOOTH. A jolly party enjoyed a picnic outing at Snaggletooth mountain last Sunday. A bounteous lunch was taken along, and the day was thoroughly enjoyed. Those participating in the affair were Mr. and Mrs. H. Marer, Mr. and Mrs. O. W Phipps and son Buster; Mrs. Loreen Snodgrass, Mr. and Mrs. George Hart and children, Mr. and Mrs. George Nay, Tim Nay, of Ledge, Calif.; Mr. and Mrs. G. S Haskin and son Stanley, Mr. T. L. Downs, Miss Irene Swarthout." We can only wish Charley had mentioned when Hutt laid out the Needles-Parker Road.

622.3 * Continue ahead (northwest). Cross cleared pavement-like area. El. 1,920 ft. (0.1).

622.4 * Continue ahead (northwest) Note dumped asphalt immediately parallel to right of Trail. Ignore road going left. El. 1,930 ft. (0.1).

622.5 * * Continue ahead (northwest) joining well traveled road coming in from right rear. Ignore several roads going left toward mountain. El. 1,920 ft (0.2).

622.7 * Continue ahead (northwest). Ignore road left. El. 1,910 ft. (0.1).

CHEMEHUEVI VALLEY

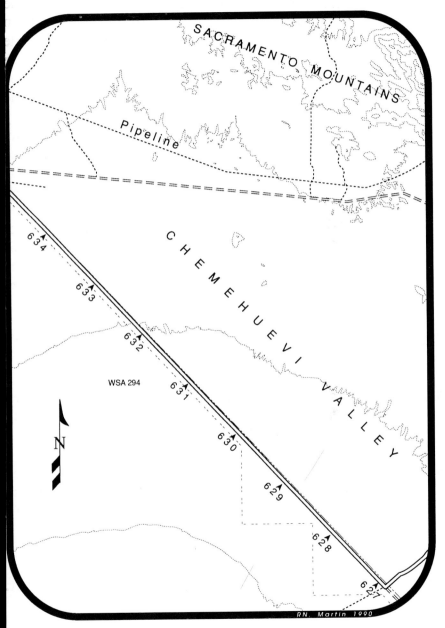

SACRAMENTO MOUNTAINS

Pipeline

CHEMEHUEVI VALLEY

634
633
632
WSA 294
631
630
629
628
62

N

RN. Martin 1990

622.8 * Trail crosses over wash 30 feet wide heade north. It parallels U.S. Highway 95, 0.5 miles away o right. El. 1,910 ft. (1.3).

623.7 Black rocks in knolls to left are bands i Precambrian gneiss, rich in biotite mica. SP.

624.1 * * Turn left (southwest) on old wagon road towar Turtle Mountains. Cairn and post. U.S. Highway 95 right 0.15 miles. El. 1,920 ft. (0.8).

624.9 * The north end of the Turtle Mountains ar visible at 11 o'clock and the Stepladder Mountains ar at 1 o'clock. El. 1,840 ft. (0.8).

625.7 * * "Y." Bear right straight (southwest). El. 1,78 ft. (0.3).

626.0 * Cairn and post on right five feet. El. 1,740 f' (0.9.

626.9 * * Turn right (northwest) on graded power lin road. Trail stays on this power line road for 14. miles. El. 1,680 ft. (8.1).

626.9 This is a line utilized by the Metropolitan Wate District to supply power for pumping water along th Colorado River Aqueduct that conveys water from Lak Havasu behind Parker Dam to the Los Angeles area. It ' another branch of the same system discussed at Mil 551.2+ in this Guide. This particular branch carrie electrical power from Hoover Dam to the pumpin stations near Parker Dam at the initial point of th

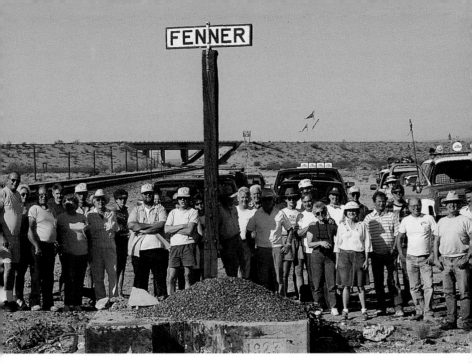

(*above*) *Friends of the Mojave Road* at Fenner.
Mile 508.3. May 6, 1989

(*below*) A caravan approaches the Piute Mountains.
About Mile 516. May 6, 1989

**Leaving Fenner, the East Mojave Heritage Trail
winds up and through the picturesque
Piute Mountains.**

(*above*) **About Mile 519.7 -- May 6, 1989**

(*right*) **About Mile 518.8 -- May 6, 1989**

(*above*) **A** **group of** *Friends of the Mojave Road*
at the monument in
Burning Shoe Wash.
Mile 530.0 -- May 6, 1989

(*right*) **The East Mojave Heritage Trail**
on its way through a wonderland
of huge granite boulders near
Sunflower Springs.
About Mile 542.2 -- May 6, 1989

(*above*)
The road can be badly eroded and rough to drive
after a rainstorm in the Old Woman Mountains.
Mile 542.6 -- February 4, 1989
Photo by Midge Davenport

(*right*)
The Old Woman Mountains were
named for the distinctive rock formation
on the horizon just left of center.
Near Mile 544 -- November 25, 1989

(*above*)
The huge bull *Ringstray* that used to be present
to greet visitors at Sunflower Springs.
Belonging to Milton Blair's Lazy Daisy Ranch,
poor *Ringstray* had to leave because, with the
passage of time, he became related to all the cows!
Mile 545.1 -- May 6, 1989

(*above right*)
Bats in a mine in the Old Woman Mountains.
Near Mile 551.2 -- November 25, 1988

(*below right*)
The "V" on west side of Turtle Mountains.
Mile 560.9 -- May 6, 1989

(*above*) **Dan Fison noses into the "narrows" in the Turtle Mountains.
Mile 571.9 -- May 6, 1989**

(*below*) **Barrel cacti are abundant in the Turtle Mountains.
They bloom in June and July.**

(*above*) Carl Volkmar and Jo Ann Smith in the "narrows."

(*below*) Donald W. Hobbs in the "narrows."

Both Mile 571.9 -- November 26, 1989

(*above*) Crossing the watershed into Gary Wash,
Turtle Mountains.
Mile 572.5 -- November 26, 1989

(*right*) A caravan in Gary Wash, Turtle Mountains.
About Mile 577 -- May 7, 1989

(*above*) **East side of Turtle Mountains.**
Mile 580.1 -- November 26, 1989

(*below*) **EMHT near Highway 95. Mopah Peaks in the background.**
Mile 585.4 -- November 26, 1989

(*above*) **On the old Needles-Parker Road.
Mile 597.0 -- May 7, 1989**

(*below*) **West Well.
Mile 606.7 -- November 26, 1989**

(*above*) Ocotillos near Sawtooth Range.
Mile 621.6 -- November 26, 1989

(*below*) Snaggle Tooth.
Mile 622.5 -- November 26, 1989

LAME DOG MINE

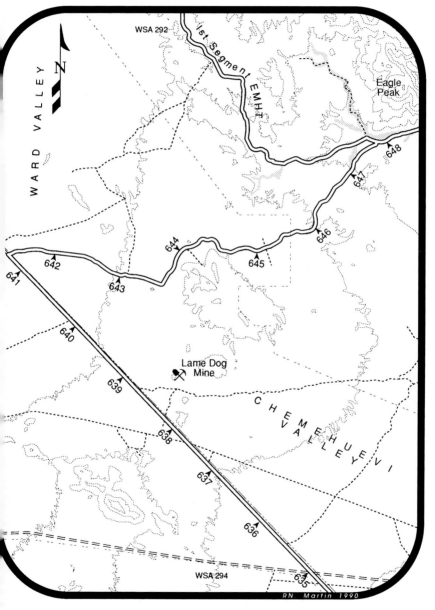

177.

Colorado River Aqueduct. It was placed in service i 1939.

631.6   Viewpoint: Stepladder Mountains acros Chemehuevi Valley at 9:00. North end of Chemehuev Mountains at 3:00. Flat Top Mountain in Sacrament Mountains just above horizon at 1:00. The Stepladde Mountains are a northern continuation of the Turtl Mountains and are similar to the Chemehuevi Mountain with a core of granodiorite that has intruded Precambria metamorphic rocks and a thin slice of volcanic rocks o the southwest side. SP.

635.0 *   **Continue ahead (northwest) on power line roac Cross gas line/telephone line road. El. 2,010 ft. (0.1)**

635.1 *   **Continue ahead (northwest) on power line roac Cross gas line road. El. 2,010 ft. (2.2).**

637.1   Brown quartz veins on right have weathered out c pinkish dacite porphyry. SP.

637.3 *   **Continue ahead (northwest) on power line roac Ignore road right to building 0.5 miles away. El. 2,14 ft. (0.4).**

637.7 *   **Continue ahead (northwest) on power line roac Ignore road left and road right to buildings. El. 2,17 ft. (0.5).**

638.1   Summit of small hill. Peak to left (southwes about 1.5 miles away has extensive desert paveme development on lower slopes (especially visible i afternoon light). Rocks on hill to right are rhyodacite breccia. Breccia is a rock composed of angular fragments, in this case pink and orange fragments in a red matrix, creating a mosaic-like appearance. SP.

8.2 *   **Continue ahead (northwest) on power line road. Ignore road right to building 0.1 mile away. El. 2,200 ft. (3.2).**

1.4 *   *   **Turn right (east) off power line road on unsigned road toward Eagle Pass in the Sacramento Mountains. Do not turn on road to magnesite mine 0.2 miles farther northwest on power line road. El. 2,030 ft. (3.0).**

3.6   Rockhound diggings on right 60 feet in chert (a form of quartz) with minor copper staining. SP.

4.4 *   *   **"Y." Bear left (northeast) to head through low hills. Right fork dead ends at mining prospect. El. 2,220 ft. (0.7).**

4.4   Entering the Sacramento Mountains. Rugged hills on right (southeast) are middle Cenozoic volcanics (about 25-30 million years old) with Precambrian metamorphics beyond. The Sacramento Mountains like other ranges we have traversed have undergone extensive detachment faulting and contain a lower plate consisting of Precambrian rocks that make up the northeastern two-thirds of the range. The upper plate contains some Precambrian rocks but is dominated by volcanics particularly along the route of the Trail. SP.

645.1 *　　　　　**Crest of pass through hills. El. 2,260 ft. (0.3)**

645.1　　　　　Dark rock on left is a basalt dike, part of a swarm of dikes in the western Sacramento Mountains. Dike swarms form under conditions of crustal stretching, which corresponds to the conditions expected from detachment faulting. SP.

645.4 *　*　**Continue ahead (east) slightly downhill. Ignore road left. El. 2,230 ft. (0.1).**

645.5 *　　　　　**Continue ahead (east) down wash in red sand wash 20 feet wide with smoke trees in it. El. 2,200 ft (0.7).**

646.2 *　　　　　**Continue ahead (east) in red sand wash. Ignore road coming in from right rear. El. 2,130 ft. (0.6).**

646.3　　　　　Reddish rock on left 30 feet is a volcanic mudflow consisting largely of dacite fragments. SP.

646.8 *　　　　　**Wonderful view of Eagle Mountain direct ahead 3 miles. El. 2,070 ft. (0.7).**

647.1　　　　　Reddish fanglomerate on right, although superficially similar to mudflow, is much younger and contains light-colored granitic and metamorphic fragments. SP.

647.2　　　　　Prominent light-colored ridge jutting out of hillside to left is a vein of travertine, (sometimes mistakenly called onyx) which is a form of calcite deposited by ancient hydrothermal spring. This hot spring would have

EAGLE PASS

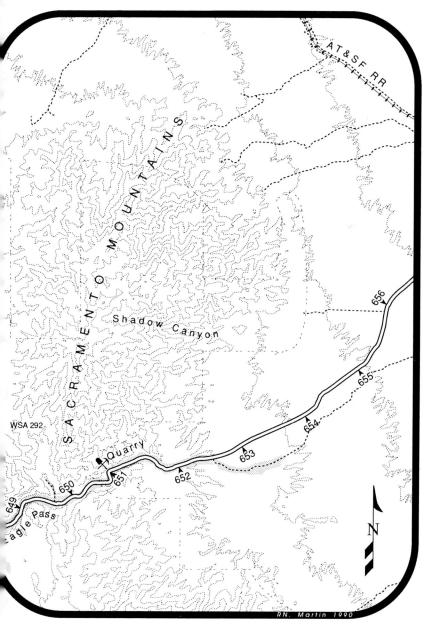

(above) Left-to-right. Skip Slavkin, Pete Panattoni,
Jo Ann Smith, Barbie Slavkin, and Tom Harris,
at the intersection of the 1st and 4th Segments
of the East Mojave Heritage Trail in the
Sacramento Mountains.
Mile 12.1 and Mile 647.9 -- Dennis Casebier Photo

(right) The East Mojave Heritage Trail
follows a smoketree wash through the
Sacramento Mountains.
3 January 1990
Dennis Casebier Photo

been active during and shortly after the period of activ volcanism. Eagle Mountain ahead on left is the remnan of a volcanic neck of intrusive latite porphyry that ha been beheaded by detachment faulting. The latite has bee dated radiometrically and assigned an age of 21.6 millio years. Hence the detachment faulting is younger than th date. SP.

647.5 *   *   "Y." Bear right (northeast) toward Eagl Mountain 0.5 miles away. El. 1,950 ft. (0.3).

647.8 *   Top of bank. El. 1,900 ft. (0.1).

647.9 *   *   Enter Eagle Pass wash 0.1 mile wide (Ea Mojave Heritage Trail Mile 12.1 -- First Segment) an continue east down the wash. Note teddy bear choll patch across wash on side of Eagle Mountain. Fror this point on into Needles you may encounter traffic o the First Segment of the East Mojave Heritage Trail it will be traveling the opposite direction. El. 1,890 f (0.4).

648.3 *   Continue east down the wash filled with smok trees through Eagle Pass. Ignore the several track coming in from the right rear. There is a good vie left of Eagle Mountain peak. El. 1,880 ft. (0.2).

648.3   DESERT LITERATURE. If you have traveled t full length of the East Mojave Heritage Trail, by this tin you have become addicted to the desert, if you weren before. You will come back again and again to this har but quiet and restful land. As the years pass you will s it change. It happens in tiny increments. A radioacti waste dump site may appear in one of your favorite valleys thereby impacting the scenery you are accustomed to. Or perhaps an area you thought would remain the same forever will become cultivated and "blossom as the rose." Or a quiet backcountry dirt road might get straightened and paved. All these things will happen -- and more. It was desert bibliographer E. I. Edwards who pointed out to me that there is only one thing about every person's desert that won't change -- the literature. Lieutenant Amiel Weeks Whipple's report, written way back in the 1850s, remains the same although the country through which he passed has changed greatly. Yet you and I can see the desert Whipple saw through the medium of his book and the illustrations in it. "Every person's desert will change, but the literature will endure," E. I. Edwards told me many years ago. "Note it in a book, that it may be for the time to come for ever and ever," he said, quoting the Bible itself. And so we have done that in these Guide books. And we are preserving the images of the desert -- written, photographic, and in various artforms -- at the Schoolhouse at Goffs. Through that effort, everyone's desert will endure to some degree. There is an essay on the subject of desert literature and the desert's bibliographer E. I. Edwards in the Appendix on pages 291 through 297.

48.5 *   Continue ahead (northeast) down wash. There is a ridge 50 feet high on the right. Eagle Mountain is 200 feet left. El. 1,820 ft. (0.5).

48.8   We have crossed the detachment fault into the lower plate comprising the core of the Sacramento Mountains. Hillside on right is gneiss with a few small basalt dikes. (Can you find them?) The greenish hue is due to chlorite, a common mineral in metamorphic rocks. SP.

649.0 *   **Continue ahead (northeast) down wash. Canyon narrows. El. 1,760 ft. (0.3).**

649.0   As the canyon narrows, spectacular cliffs appear on both sides of the Trail. A good reference point for the line of contact between the existing intrusives above and the metamorphic rocks below can be seen in the form of an elongated cave (a ledge cave). JV.

649.2   Look up steep hillside on left and see trace of detachment fault which is the contact between the pink latite and the underlying greenish gneisses. SP.

649.3 *   **Continue ahead northeast through the canyon. Ruins of a wooden flume once used to carry "picture rock" down the hillside are on the rocky slope to the right. Eagle Peak rises above the canyon walls to the left. This area is called Eagle Pass, although it is not at the crest or summit of the mountains. El. 1,720 ft. (0.4).**

649.4   Note small arch to left of flat notch at top of cliff on left. Also note columnar cooling joints in cliff, which are bent in places indicating movement of the intrusive mass before cooling was complete. SP.

649.7 *   **Continue ahead (south). Ignore road left. El. 1,700 ft. (1.3).**

9.8   Look left upslope at 9:00 to see gold prospect just below base of cliff. Detachment fault is at base of cliff. Rocks in the lower plate are extensively shattered and metamorphosed especially near the fault contact. This shattering has allowed mineralized fluids given off by hot magma to permeate the rock and deposit minerals. This new understanding of mineral deposits in the region has radically changed prospecting throughout the region of California, Arizona, and Nevada which has been affected by detachment faulting. SP.

1.0 *   Continue ahead (northeast). Extensive rock quarry on the left. The rock here is used in Colorado River dikes. Heavy equipment may be in use here. El. 1,600 ft. (1.2).

1.0   The quarried rock represents highly metamorphosed rock. Note that the rock that is being presently dug is quite green in color -- metamorphosed rock that has been "baked" by extreme heats and pressures for a long geologic period of time making the original rock now much harder and more resistant. Next to granite, this type of stone is commonly used in river dikes because of its high resistance to weathering. JV.

2.2 *   Continue ahead (east). Extensive cholla along road. El. 1,400 ft. (0.1).

2.2   Large pale green (almost white) outcrop 30 inches on right is gneiss which has been severely sheared and altered by detachment faulting. The shiny faces are slickensides -- surfaces along which movement has occurred. Rocks seen along the Trail for the next 0.4

NEEDLES

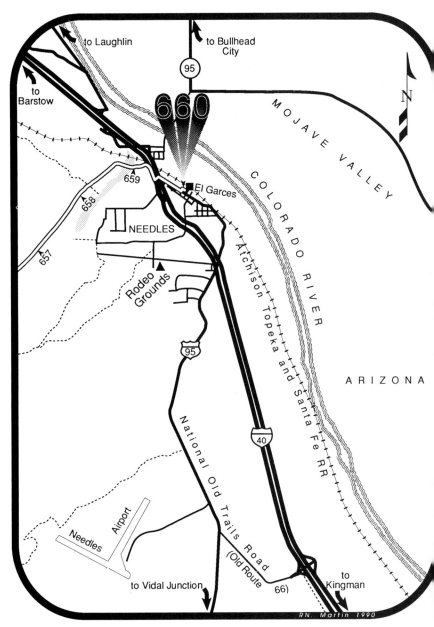

miles have been similarly affected. These are often referred to by geologists as "really messed up rocks." SP.

2.3 *   Continue ahead (east) crossing flood control berm and entering graded road. El. 1,390 ft. (0.2).

2.5 *   Continue ahead (east) crossing larger flood control berm. El. 1,380 ft. (5.7).

8.2 *   Continue ahead (northeast). Ignore road that crosses. El. 630 ft. (0.3).

8.5 *   Continue ahead (northeast) through trash dump area. Trail bends left and right descending into wash. El. 560 ft. (0.3).

8.8 *   Continue ahead (east) across wash. Ignore roads left and right in area. El. 500 ft. (0.1).

8.9 *   Cross berm on far side of wash staying on main wide gravel road. El. 490 ft. (0.1).

9.0 *   Continue ahead (east) on a paved road with a building 200 feet right signed "C.P. National." Be sure you are no longer in four-wheel drive. El. 480 ft. (0.1).

9.1 *   Continue ahead on paved road with Union 76 oil tanks on left. Paved Trail will bear right (south) soon. El. 480 ft. (0.4).

9.5 *   *   Turn left (northeast) on L Street. You are back in the city of Needles, California. El. 480 ft. (0.1).

659.6 * *   **Pass under I-40 and turn right (southeast) on Broadway Street. El. 480 ft. (0.3).**

659.9 * *   **Turn left (northeast) on G Street. El. 475 ft. (0.1).**

660.0 * *   **Turn right (southeast) on Front Street a short distance to the cannon in the park left. Pull up and park on the right. Turn your engine off. You have completed the EAST MOJAVE HERITAGE TRAIL. El. 475 ft.**

660.0   Needles came into existence as a railroad town in 1883 when the Atlantic and Pacific Railroad was built from the east and the Southern Pacific Railroad was built from the west. Today the composite of these two railroads constitute the main line of the Atchison, Topeka, and Santa Fe Railway Company.

Needles takes its name from three sharp peaks south of Topock, Arizona, at the eastern end of the Mohave Mountain range. They were given this name by Lt. Amiel Weeks Whipple in 1854. "The Needles" are across the Colorado River in Arizona.

For many years Needles was thought of as only a railroad town. But that was true only in the earlier years. It soon became the supply point for prospectors, homesteaders, miners, and others attempting to eke a living out of the interior of the desert. As the automobile became an instrument of transcontinental travel, beginning in earnest in about 1910, Needles became a highway town. At first it was called the National Old Trails Road, then it became U. S. Highway 66, and today it is Interstate Highway 40. Needles is home to many of the

Mojave Indians who are residents of the Fort Mojave Indian Reservation. The town site is part of their ancestral lands.

Today the tri-state area of the Colorado River Valley from Laughlin southward to Needles is undergoing explosive growth and development. We can only hope that Needles will retain its character as an old time railroad town, river town, highway town, focal point of the adjoining desert, and home to the Mojave Indians

SANTA FE BRIDGE OVER COLORADO RIVER

191.

The Train Depot and Harvey House was important to
Needles through much of its history. El Garces *(above)*
was completed in 1908. The older structure *(below)* had
burned in 1906. Richard D. McCutchan Collection.

(above) Steamboats and ferries were an important part of
the Needles scene. Richard D. McCutchan Collection.
(below) This auto bridge was completed in 1916 thereby
assuring Needles' future as a highway town.
Alice (Zimmerman) Brownfield Collection.

Scenes from 7IL Ranch in the late 1920s.
(above) Mark Pettit and Bob working cattle.
(below) Mark Pettit in front of building that is still in use.
Betty (Pettit) Papierski Collection

APPENDIX

....

....

.....

....

...

..

.

THE 7IL RANCH
by Elizabeth (Pettit) Papierski

We bought the ranch in 1927. Close to the Providence Mountains and surrounded by hills and mesas, what few buildings there were blended in with the greasewood and yucca making little impact upon the landscape. We had running water in the kitchen with a stream about as big as your finger. A big wood stove, a sink, cupboards and a large square table in one corner.

The kitchen was the gathering place, the dining room, family room and work room. There was a smaller room used for storage, especially for beef wrapped in tarps to keep it cool and fresh. We built a porch around two sides of the house and started another room that was never completed and always remained open to the elements. We had our beds on the porch all year around. Sometimes to make room for company, Bob and I moved our cots out onto the ground, covered with tarps we sometimes woke to find an inch of snow on top of us.

Away from the house was a blacksmith shop, a

195.

huge watering trough, a two room storage house, a new hay barn and a rock wall to the west side of the area. Among these buildings were many corrals and branding pens. Altogether this was home for my father Mark Pettit, mother Mary, sister Barbara [Bob] and myself, Betty.

My sister and I were not the boys my Dad wanted so we became tomboys. We wore long underwear, flannel shirts, bib overalls, heavy wool socks and sturdy boys' work shoes. In summer the less we had on the better.

An almond tree grew just off the porch, it provided pleasant shade and seemed to be the greenest thing on the ranch. Mother did have a small vegetable garden on the west side of the house kept alive with the water from the sink. She always grew castor bean bushes, which provided a look of green around the house.

We always had a few chickens scratching around the garden and woodpile, providing a roast chicken once or twice a year and a steady supply of eggs. Sometimes we had a cow tame enough to milk but most of the time it was good old canned milk. There was always plenty to eat, hearty fare tho' it was. Oat meal, beans, biscuits, beefsteak, canned tomatoes and peaches, jerky gravy on pancakes, rice pudding and sometimes a pan of fudge or a lemon cake.

Our cattle were Herefords which roamed far and wide staying close enough to the waterholes to reach them every day or so. The total amount of cattle we owned varied from two hundred to four hundred and fifty. It was a small herd but the area could only support so many.

To get firewood we would take the Ford truck and go way up into the Providence Mountains where the pinon pine grew. We would gather the dead and down wood laying around. Those were great trips. We would be high enough to have a sweeping view of the desert and there were hidden springs with thick green grass growing near them. We would build a small fire and cook our supper and not get home till way after dark. Once in a while we made beds on the ground and stayed all night.

Life was never dull, from the time when I made the breakfast biscuits when I was six years old and put too much baking soda in them and they came out of the oven GREEN. Or the time Old Jim [Craig] was shooting at a hawk up by the cliffs above the house and with a loud twang and rattle he hit a strand of barbed wire fence which in turn recoiled and wrapped around the horns of a big horn sheep. My Dad and Jim had to climb up there and cut the wire away and let him go.

My Dad came across a baby coyote and brought him home and tried to tame him. He fed, petted it using gloves, talked to it and thought he was going to have a new pet. When he thought it was tame enough one day he let it loose, it immediately bit my father and took off like a streak of lightning. My dad was furious. But the pup was gone.

Bobbie had a small dog named Skipper and it was her constant companion, even when she went riding. One day two mine promoters came to the ranch looking for information and when they left they backed over Skipper. He was still alive but in bad shape. Bob told the men to leave, went into the house and got her rifle and took Skipper to the hay barn and shot him. It was one of the sad days.

Mother had a grapevine growing on the porch that was her pride and joy. She always got a few grapes every year which she shared with us and we made a celebration out of it. One day one of the horses got through the fence and started to nibble on the vine. Mother exploded! I never saw her move so fast, she grabbed the broom and went after that horse like a small hurricane. Needless to say the fence got fixed immediately.

Old Jim Craig came on the scene soon after we moved to the ranch. He attached himself to my dad and seemed to be around ever after. He had a lot of relatives who kept him bothered and busy, and who appeared at the ranch from time to time. I remember Bert and Al, his brothers. Al couldn't speak above a whisper.

Old Jim was a tough little desert rat who never seemed to get tired and was always willing to pitch in and help with the worst jobs. He was the one who started calling my sister Bob, we called her Bob for the rest of her life. He was also the one who said I could have a horse of my own whenever Old Kelso (Kelso was a 20 year old gelding) had a colt! We turned Kelso out to pasture about that time and he would show up at the ranch gate and wait to have new shoes put on once or twice a year. Well, I got the last laugh on Jim when Kelso showed up with a young colt that was marked just like him. It had lost its mother and had taken up with Kelso. They gave him to me, swayback, pot belly and all.

The water holes and springs and wells were vital lifeline for cattle and people. There was Colton Wells, Adams, Whiskey Spring, Gilroy, Goldstone, Cave Springs, and Government Holes. There were names such as Hole-in-the-Wall, Winston Basin, Wild Horse Mesa, The Speckled Pup Mine, Fenner Spring Mine, Vontrigger, Black Canyon, Beecher, Barbar, and Silver King that were part of the vocabulary if you lived on the 7IL.

Throw in the names of people like Joe Larieo, George Harper Wishards, Alexander, Dorr, Craig, Murphy, Halsell, Joe Bolyn, Nick Loco, Joe Spencer, Wilson, Yoakum, Talbot, Thorndyke Ralph Swing, Ben Wallace, and Frank Amos and you have a few of the old timers that made their way to our ranch.

Many others came out from San Bernardino, Barstow, and Los Angeles to prospect and promote mines; some came just to "rough it" and ride horses and eat Mother's beans, biscuits and beefsteak. No matter how many were there she always offered a hospitable attitude; after cooking their breakfast she would get on a horse and ride twenty-five miles to round up some stray cattle or run-away horse. On top of this Mother had asthma, caused from horses and dust. She often spent time in bed suffering to get her breath. She was diminutive with big blue eyes, blonde curly hair, and a great sense of humor. When I think back, I know everyone loved Mary Pettit.

The most frightening event that happened at the ranch (to me) was the great electrical storm of 1931. Mother, Bob, and I were alone at the ranch. The dark clouds had been on the horizon all afternoon and the wind picked up just before dark, howling down upon us, rattling the tin roof and screaming around the corners. Thunder and lightning started about dark, booming around the hills nearby. We decided to all sleep together in Mother's bed on the porch which was open and looked down onto the desert to the south.

The storm increased in intensity as the rain started. The lightning was blinding in its energy making a dazzling, ghastly constant blue light, striking yucca plants and turning them into blazing torches of yellow fires. The thunder claps were so close there was no space between them. It crashed and boomed and rolled across the sky like the biggest war in history was being waged. We three huddled together with fear and awe. Suddenly one gigantic thunder bolt split the night and we thought we were hit. It was close, it was our blacksmith shop, which burned to the ground that night. Suddenly through the storm we saw two little eyes of light that did not falter and came on until we realized it was an automobile. It was Old Jim, coming home with his little white dog. We piled out of bed and rushed to greet him, not knowing how much it helped just to have someone else there with us.

CAMP CLIPPER
AND THE
DESERT TRAINING CENTER

by Ev Hayes

In early 1942 the War Department sent General George S. Patton to set up the Desert Training Center in the "vast unoccupied area of the desert in Southern California." After arriving at Indio, Patton flew over the area, south to El Centro and north to Searchlight, and from the Colorado River west to Twenty Nine Palms. While in the air, Patton pointed to the ground and to his maps and directed that a camp be built here and there. He identified eight camps in California, one of which was Camp Clipper. Others were called Ibis, Iron Mountain, Granite, Coxcomb, Rice (actually an Army Airfield), Pilot Knob, and the Headquarters for the Desert Training Center, Camp Young. The training area eventually extended into Arizona and was renamed the California Arizona Maneuver Area (CAMA); however, General Patton's involvement was limited to the original Desert Training Center, or DTC.

The original concept behind the DTC was to create a fictitious theater of operations using Los Angeles as the invasion point. In addition to training men under conditions as close to combat as possible, the Army wanted to test supply, communication, and transportation routes to see just how far they could be stretched and still function. Even though Patton's personal involvement only lasted from March to July of 1942, the DTC/CAMA continued to grow and was not officially closed until midnight, April 30, 1944 because of a shortage of support

(above) Leo J. Panattoni standing by the
placard for
Company "F" of the 15th Cavalry.
At Camp Coxcomb -- Desert Training Center.
Winter of 1943-1944.
Leo Panattoni Collection

(left) Street Scene at Camp Clipper.
Anti Tank Company,
136th Infantry, 33rd Division.
James D. Bryant Collection

troops to sustain the men in training. While estimates vary, at least one million troops trained at one time or another during the existence of the DTC/CAMA.

For almost forty years the camps lay abandoned and unknown except to a few locals and members of organizations like the Council on America's Military Past. In 1984, anticipating the upcoming fortieth anniversary of Victory in Europe (VE) Day, the Needles Office of the BLM began to research the location and extent of camps associated with the DTC. What began as a modest effort became a national campaign when the *Los Angeles Times* did a story in November, 1984 on the Bureau's effort to write an interpretive plan for the Iron Mountain Camp. National wire services picked up the story and headlines all over the country read "U.S. SEEKS PATTON VETERANS!" The Needles office was listed as the place to write and soon the letters began pouring in. In all, over 750 letters were received from over 45 states! The remainder of this story relies heavily on information gathered from the many proud veterans who served in the DTC.

Patton chose the locations of all camps so that they were near rail transportation or sources of water. One Patton legend was born when he appeared before the Metropolitan Water District of Southern California (MWD) in early 1942 regarding water from their aqueduct to serve some of the camps. After hearing about his anticipated needs, the MWD announced that they would consider his request and could probably render a decision in a few months. General Patton politely (?) informed them that he had started using water that very day and just wanted the MWD to know that he had done so, his schedule for training troops did not allow for bureaucratic delay!

The Santa Fe Railroad provided most of the transportation in and out of the DTC. Fred Robinson, now of Fair Oaks, California, was Yardmaster for the Southern Pacific Railroad at Colton during the war. He relates:

"Camp Ono [not one of the actual DTC camps] was built about three miles north of San Bernardino on the Santa Fe Railroad. It was here that most of the supplies were loaded in box cars, flat cars, or any other type cars that were needed. In the meantime, an Army Transportation Office was opened and located in the Colton City Park. This office played a big role in moving the supplies such as seeing that way bills and manifest bills were delivered at the time of the interchange of loaded cars from Santa Fe to Southern Pacific [or the reverse] at Colton. Sometimes Army troops were sent to guard some of the cars in case they had to be set out [put on a siding] enroute. As many as 50 to 80 cars each night were forwarded to the Desert [Training] Center for General Patton's troops."

The main off loading point into the DTC was the siding called Freda, on State Highway 62, approximately three miles west of Rice, California. While men were sent to camps throughout the DTC, most write and reflect on arriving at Freda to begin their time in the desert.

Walter H. Smith, an electrician for the Pullman Company during the war and now retired in Los Angeles, California, recalls firsthand how troops were moved in and out of the DTC:

"I was an electrician for the Pullman Co. and participated in moving the 1st, 3rd, 5th, 7th and 9th

Armored Divisions in and out of the training areas. The normal procedure was an in and out move, i.e., after the first groups had completed their initial and final desert training. I was stationed at Freda [siding] near Danby Dry Lake for the first troop move. I was there one month -- it took 600 pullman cars to move one division (15,000 men) in and then the electricians of the Pullman Co. and other railway men would check all the cars and clean them and have them ready in a few hours to move another trainload of troops out. Sometimes the schedule was 3 trains a day. It varied according to requirements. During the time between arrivals and departures, I used to watch the Army transportation specialists practice various ways of loading tanks and guns at 20 tons each and all kinds of equipment on flat cars for transportation to the ships. They would put 48 or so flat cars on a siding and have a loading ramp at one end only. Take 20 ton guns for instance! They would lift (manually) 2 jeeps on the flat cars and then use a cat with a pushing arm to push the guns up the ramp - then the two jeeps were attached to the gun to steer it down 47 flat cars as one or two prime mover trucks pulled it by running beside the car with cable attached to the gun carriage. They tried several ways, in addition, but they didn't prove satisfactory.

"The railway workers had to depend on the Army cook cars to obtain food for the first few days till a commissary was set up for them and due to the intense sand storms your food had plenty of sand in it... ...Freda was the largest of Patton's training areas [four camps, Rice, Iron Mountain, Granite, and Coxcomb were in close proximity] and was three miles from Rice - on the Santa Fe Branch to Blythe - the main by-pass line ran from Cadiz to Parker and on to Phoenix - this was the route the

(above) Mail call and *(below)* chow time at the
Desert Training Center.
Both photos Winter of 1943-1944.
Both photos Leo Panattoni Collection

troops took in and out of Freda. When Freda was closed, everything (not tanks or guns) was buried in a bulldozed trench on north side of camp. I was at all major troop moves for 1942, 1943, 1944....

"At Goffs there was an ammo dump on the way in from the main highway and there was also a military hospital with nurses (female) there. The gunnery range was on a mountain just north of the railroad into Needles. We usually went into Needles once a week for a shower and slept at Goffs in a pullman car parked with a rail taken out so they wouldn't move it. At Freda I slept in a bed on a trailer floor -- no water -- no food -- just heat...

"Rice had what was supposed to be the longest bar-counter in the USA. With 160,000 troops they had only this bar. It consisted of three buildings as I remember -- the bar had a huge desert type cooler, mounted 50 feet from the end of the bar on a tower with a large pipe to carry cool air directly down the length of the bar. I think the bar was 180 feet long. That was the only business in Rice except the railroad."

Think of the men that arrived at Freda and were assigned to one or another of the camps. Most were from the East and had never imagined a place like the California Desert could even exist. H.J. "Jack" Meany of Rolling Hills, CA relates the following:

"Our first camp was set up at Goffs [in May of 1942] where we were limited to the use of one shelter half (a piece of dark canvas about 3' x 7') for protection against the sun and blowing sand. We tied these to the sagebrush and rocks about 2' above the ground and then laid under them on a dark wool blanket. The radiation off the dark canvas was almost as intense as the sun itself so comfort was a relative term. Large refrigerated boxes on wheels were brought in to cool and rehydrate those overcome by the heat, physical exertion and lack of water. They were placed on racks in these boxes, much as in a morgue, for about 24 hours, or until their body temperature dropped to subnormal for a few hours, and most were then able to return to duty..."

Soon after arrival, the common verse exchanged among the troops became:

The men that trained in the desert
are sure to go to heaven
Because they have done their stretch in hell!

To get an idea of what made up a World War II Armored Division and the complexity of moving the mass of men (15,000+) and equipment, Samuel A. Schenker, Sr., of Sharon, PA supplied the following list of units that made up the Fourth Armored Division while training in the desert:

8th, 35th and 37th Tank Battalions
10th, 51st and 53rd Armored Infantry Battalions
22nd, 66th and 94th Armored Field Artillery Battalions
24th Armored Engineer Battalion
25th Calvary Reconnaissance Squadron, Mechanized
126th Armored Ordnance Maintenance Battalion
46th Armored Medical Battalion
Headquarters and Headquarters Battery, Division Artillery
CCA Headquarters and Headquarters Company
CCB Headquarters and Headquarters Company
Reserve Command
Division Headquarters Company
144th Signal Company

Trains Headquarters and Headquarters Company
Forward Echelon, Fourth Armored Headquarters
4th Armored Division Military Police Platoon
4th Armored Division Band
504th CounterIntelligence Corps Detachment
704th Tank Destroyer Battalion
489th Anti-Aircraft Artillery Battalion
3804th and 444th Quartermaster Truck Company
995th Engineer Treadway Bridge Company
696th Armored Field Artillery Battalion
1st Platoon 16th Field Hospital
456th Ambulance Company
5th Detachment, 166th Signal Photo Company
Interrogation of Prisoner of War Teams Number 56 & 61

When it is considered that at least 20 Army Divisions trained in the desert, the immensity of the operation is obvious. Benjamin W. Martin of Barstow, California, relates what it was like when he was a radio communications specialist with the Fourth Armored Division during a maneuver:

"I don't know if most people can imagine how big an Armored Division is. About three a.m. one night [morning] we were awakened by tanks roaring by. It was the Fourth Armored going out on a problem. They roared by continually and by noon the last unit went by. That's a lot of vehicles. But the deserts are so vast there were two Armored Divisions and two Motorized Divisions out there in the desert all at one time and you could drive all day long in one direction and not see any vehicle or sign of human beings around at all."

Vehicles were essential to most maneuvers during the war. Walter R. Hennessey of Providence, Rhode

Island, submitted letters he had written home during the war and that had been kept by his mother all these years. Walter, an enlisted man, was known as "Three Star Hennessey" because he always signed his name followed by three stars. One letter in particular is interesting to most of us who depend on vehicles, especially as it relates to gas mileage. This letter is dated February 1, 1942:

"...I am going to try and tell you the general outline of our equipment and activity out here in the golden west. The family desires such information I imagine. So please discuss it with them...

"First our company [Company B 757th Tank Battalion] is divided into four separate parts, namely headquarters, first, second and third platoons. I personally am in the second. Headquarters are the truck drivers, peep [jeep] drivers, mechanics, clerks, etc. The three platoons are made up of tank crews. Each platoon has five tanks. Therefore, counting command tanks our company strength is eighteen tanks. Our battalion has three tank companies as well as a headquarters company. Each company has one half-ton truck, four peeps [jeeps], one scout car and five two and one half ton trucks so you may see that when the whole battalion is strung out on the road at intervals of fifty yards quite a few miles are taken. This large convoy doesn't hold up traffic unless it is trying to cross the route. The convoy on march travels between forty and forty-five with stops for checks.

"My main concern is naturally tanks so therefore I shall try to explain them. Before I forget a tank gets two miles on a gallon of gas, the trucks about eight, scout cars about four, peeps [jeeps] about the same as civilian cars so you can see now where the tax payer's money goes.

"Our tanks are all light tanks (M-3) weighing

211.

fourteen tons, medium tanks weigh approximately 25 tons, heavy tanks forty tons. Germany has an eighty ton, Russia a ninety, and the USA a sixty ton tank but these are entirely too heavy and clumsy.

"I shall only talk about the light tanks. These tin cans are approximately the same length as an automobile with armor plate of one and three quarter inches in most places. The engine is a Continental airplane engine of 250 horsepower and seven cylinders using six gallons [of oil] when changed.

"At present our vehicles are one third loaded with ammunition this being 3500 rounds of thirty caliber machine gun bullets, and 31 shells for the 37 mm gun. Both these guns are accurate up to about 1200 yards but are capable of doing damage at much greater distances. In fact the 37 mm shell is dangerous up to seven miles. The pressure behind the explosion of the 37 mm is 36,000 pounds or 18 ton so you may see why this baby can do so much damage.

"Tank formations are very similar to those of the [Army] Air Force, column, line, wedge, etc. These formations are done to precision and are either directed from radio or flag commands. There are many minor details such as stripping, cleaning, repairing, and knowing all the parts and functions of all guns. I think everyone shall agree this is quite a feat for a crew of four."

Most of the hundreds of veterans that wrote about their experience in the desert didn't dwell on their time at a particular camp as they moved about constantly and weren't told much about their specific location. Many letters relate to trips taken while on passes to Needles, Las Vegas, Palm Springs, and the Los Angeles Basin. Vincent Fazio of Yucaipa, California, remembers his experience with the Sixth Armored Division and it is typical of most of the letters from veterans who served in the DTC. Mr. Fazio's recollections begin with the train trip across the United States from the East Coast:

"Once the wheels started turning, time virtually stood still save for the kitchen crews and KPs [men temporarily assigned kitchen duty], toting their big pots of chow down the aisle of one car after another, ladling contents into mess kits and canteen cups. Occasional stops gave welcome opportunity to stretch stiff legs. Well out into the plains states, winding up the endless slope towards the Continental Divide, passengers could see, miles and miles ahead, the smoke from a half-dozen similar trains, spaced out miles apart and all headed west. Passing trains were few and far between; occasionally, ours would 'take siding' and let a heavily laden trainload of vital war materials thunder past with as many as two monstrous locomotives at the head, a couple cut into the middle and another couple pushing from the rear.

"Then one afternoon our train was switched off the main line and rolled down a branch. Close to the tracks, headed in the opposite direction, clouds of dust kicked up by their tracks, a column of tanks pitched and rolled over the undulating sands. We knew we were about 'there' -- wherever 'there' was! Soon we were to learn about places like Rice and Freda and Grommet, Needles and Yuma. But now it was dark; we were in the middle of nowhere. Vehicles were rolled down the ramp at an unloading dock and parked; officers and men were guided to a place where they could unroll sleeping bags or blankets, fit their contours into the sand and drop off into slumber under the stars -- a slumber broken now and then by a shrieking soldier who discovered a snake seeking warm company.

213.

(above) A light M-5 Tank and a motorcycle
(below) are tested against the sand dunes
of the Desert Training Center. October 1942.
U. S. Army Photos

The machinery of war at the Desert Training Center.
(above) Danby rail siding. Dick MacPherson Collection
(below) Tank park at Freda. U. S. Army Photo

"Daybreak introduced a new and strange experience in a new and strange environment. Far away lay the horizon, marked to the north by treeless, jagged mountains of a varying hue. Elsewhere, sparse desert greenery that, due to perspective and long, gradual slopes, blended into a variety of pastel shades. All-pervading was the wind and the strange, pungent odor of greasewood.

"Open space quickly was transformed into the usual orderly military array of canvas. Sand, of course, was everywhere. After some weeks truckload after truckload of plasterboard materialized from a gypsum processing plant some miles away; laid on smoothed-out sand, it floored the tents after a fashion. Troops got into the habit of shaking out their boots in the morning to evict possible desert denizens, and to secure small belongings from larcenous desert rats.

"They learned to drive slowly within the populated areas -- especially near the kitchens -- to hold down the dust; elsewhere, to head across the sands or beside the roads, few paved. The directive was to stay off the roads, presumably to save them from the wear and tear of tracked vehicles, or to get us accustomed to cross-country driving, or both. Whatever the reason, it eventually took its toll in broken springs and other vehicular damage.

"It was hot when we arrived, and for a few weeks thereafter, the burlap-screened Quartermaster-serviced open air shower facility a few miles from camp enjoyed great patronage -- but only for a few weeks. October, we found, brought its own brand of dry but freezing weather. A No. 10 can of water set on top of the stove sufficed for a washcloth bath. Canvas water bags hung on a peg outside the tent became solid ice overnight. It was a wise practice to start the day in multiple layers of clothing and shed gradually as the sun climbed higher. The knit, tiny-visored skull caps designed to be worn under the helmet liner were cozy, with the ear flaps turned down.

"Hissing gasoline lanterns provided light for friendly card games or private reading during the night hours. Or, beer bottle in hand, one could squat on the hard sand and watch a movie shown on a fabric screen that billowed in the wind, producing a funhouse mirror-like image of the heroes and heroines, villains and villainesses. And woe to the GI who tavern keeper Ray Rahn caught throwing away an empty beer bottle. 'We had to turn in a case of empty bottles for every full case we got,' a mellowed Rahn explained at a later date."

Camp Clipper was actually two camps named for their proximity to the Clipper Mountains. Flying over the area it appears that one camp was poorly located in major washes and was only occupied until the first flash flood. There is also a well preserved military airfield to the east of the camp. During my years in Needles many people told me the camp was actually called Essex, after the town, but both official Army records and the veterans who wrote about their specific experience at Clipper make no reference to a Camp Essex. Camp Clipper is identical to all the other camps in that it is constructed around a flag circle with company streets radiating outward. However, three things are unique to Clipper. First are the yuccas lining the main street, another is the circular water cistern and adjacent wells, and last is the amphitheater. Although I have not been able to find official documentation, Clipper is supposed to be the place where Italian Prisoners of War were interred near the close of the DTC and may have been used to pick up unexploded ordnance in the area.

At least two Infantry Divisions trained at Clipper. The 33rd Infantry Division (a National Guard Division from Illinois) and the 93rd Infantry Divisions (one of only two divisions in World War II made up of entirely of black fighting men).

Hugh Jennings of Campbell, California, served with the 33rd Infantry Division at Clipper and recalls:

"That was a long time ago... ...I'll never forget how wonderfully peaceful the evenings were with their calmness and coolness after the heat (110 degrees+) and winds of each day. It was at that time that I learned the meaning of the phrase we sing in America telling about purple mountain majesty...

"Our camp was called Camp Clipper after a mountain or range in the area called Clipper. We were quite close to Highway 66 about 40 miles west of Needles... ...During the final five weeks of my stay in the desert, my wife, Molly, managed to find a place to stay in Palm Springs and I was able to negotiate that distance each weekend by way of a desert road through Essex, Amboy, Dry Lake, 29 Palms and quite a few Joshua trees...

"One other item I recall about my desert experience was a brief session we were given concerning the various varmints of the area. A naturalist, who, of course, was familiar with such things, tried to show us the difference between poisonous and non-poisonous snakes and also tried to assure us that scorpions were not quite as venomous as their reputation. The purpose of these teachings was to remove fear of our surroundings. As with most situations I faced during five years of war, I decided it's better to make the most of them and not fight them. I forced myself to pick up a large King snake while on a field exercise. Of course, I wasn't satisfied until I was sure my Colonel was well indoctrinated too -- I slipped it into his desk as a surprise!"

Another veteran who trained at Clipper was Arthur Wills, now a retired postal worker living in Los Angeles. Before the war Arthur served in a CCC camp at Lake Elsinore, California, and remembers fighting fires from Elsinore to Santa Barbara. During World War II he served at Clipper with the 93rd Infantry Division and recalls marching from Clipper to Las Vegas on numerous occasions:

"We had night maneuvers with other Divisions. It was hot in the day and cold at night. Conditions were as if you were in combat. We walked from 6 in the morning until 6 at night. There were a lot of Infantry Divisions training in all those camps, not just Patton's tanks. We had flash floods. It was nothing to wake up in water and mud, all cold and wet. The sun would dry you out and bake the mud on your clothes."

While not actually at Clipper, another veteran wrote about his experience while stationed in Needles with the 3rd Finance Disbursing Section. Greg Corken of Dubuque, Iowa, relates:

"On arrival in Needles [February 6, 1943] we were assigned for rations and quarters to the 128th Evacuation Hospital. The hospital was located on a sandy flat on the east side of Needles on the roadway leading to Blythe. In about a week we were transferred to the west side of the city where the Army Engineers were giving the finishing touches to two hospitals...

"The Desert [finance] Headquarters was at Banning so my travels took me to that area which included Palm Springs, Palm Desert, Indio, and Twentynine Palms. It was a long and hot and dusty all day drive to make the round trip at 35 mph. In addition, we made jeep trips daily to nearby towns including Goffs, which was the railhead for the Needles area of the DTC.

"Everything in the area was temporary, built to represent a war zone facility by the Army Engineers, and intended to make the entire area independent and self-sufficient, including a water supply and stand-pipe. All buildings and tents were camouflaged to appear from the air as a part of the City of Needles. We were not dependent on the city or civilians for anything except the convenience of their bank, their stores, and their recreation and sociability, which was most generous and excellent. The good people of Needles and the Elks in particular, in my opinion, tolerated a lot of inconvenience in those days."

A final excerpt from the many letters submitted reflects one of the lesser known but nonetheless real happenings associated with the DTC:

"Another event, true to life but a little seedy, involved a squaw at one of the sites who became known among the soldiers as Squaw Cactus Flower. She had a pickup truck that was apparently used for hauling old car parts because it had a lot of sandy oil and grease on the pickup floor [bed]. Cactus Flower would turn a trick on the greasy truck bed for a can of beer purchased at a highway bar. Greasy, grimy uniforms became the mark of true swordsmen among the wearers and their peers. Cactus Flower was drinking a lot of beer on those hot summer nights, but then new appearances of greasy uniforms stopped abruptly. Again, the rumor mill had the reason: the officers had washed the sand and grease out of the truck bed and she was now drinking their beer with no

(above) Half-tracks of the 5th Armored Division move
forward across the desert.
(below) 5th Armored Division Camp at the DTC.
October 1942 -- U. S. Army Photos

telltale soiled uniforms to prove it. There was also speculation that Squaw Cactus Flower caused more men to be put in the refrigerated boxes than the heat and rigors of maneuvers."

While the early purpose of the Desert Training Center may have been to get troops ready for the invasion of North Africa, the eventual purpose was to train and harden troops for all fronts. Units from the Desert Training Center fought in Europe, the Pacific, and even the Aleutian Islands. Since the DTC was only a piece of the global conflict then underway, information about the men and women who served in the DTC has had to come from the very people who served there.

According to the Army's official record of the DTC, the training to be undertaken in the desert would include:

1. Operations with restricted water supply
2. Sustained operations remote from railheads
3. Operating in dispersed combat groups during which constant threat of hostile air and mechanized attack would be simulated
4. Speed in combat supply, particularly refueling and ammo
5. Supply under cover of darkness
6. Desert navigation for all personnel
7. Laying and removal of mine fields by all personnel
8. Maintenance and evacuation of motor vehicles
9. Special features of sanitation, hygiene and first aid
10. Combined training with the Army Air Forces

There was a moment in the history of the DTC when it seemed the troops there might be drawn precipitously into the defense of the Pacific Coast. From May 31, 1942 through June 7, 1942 all units in DTC were placed on full alert due to suspected invasion threat on the West Coast. California was "troop poor" at the beginning of the war, the DTC comprised the largest number of troops available for thousands of miles. The alert was canceled after the United States scored a resounding victory over the Japanese at the Battle of Midway.

A little advertised purpose for the DTC was testing of new equipment. Over 225 separate items ranging from heavy tanks to combat boots were issued and used by the troops before general distribution to the rest of the services.

All that remains of Camp Clipper is the round water cistern, the yucca lined main street, and row upon row of rocks outlining tent and assembly areas, broken pieces of dishes and other rusted paraphernalia speaking of residents long gone. Interstate 40 cuts through a part of the camp with a small portion laying to the north of the freeway and the remainder to the south. As you wander the once crowded area, imagine what the soldiers of World War II must have experienced having for the most part arrived from the East.

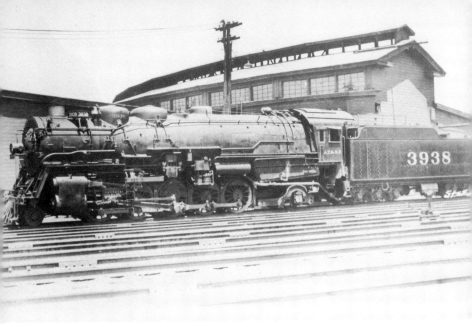

Atchison, Topeka, & Santa Fe Railroad
engines pictured at Needles.
(above) Steele's Photo Service Collection
(below) Kansas State Historical Society

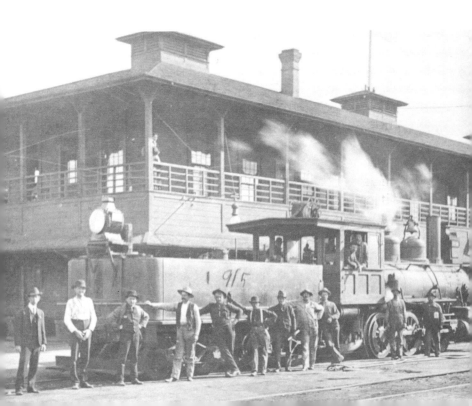

THE SANTA FE RAILROAD
IN THE EAST MOJAVE

By Delmer G. Ross
Professor of History, Loma Linda University

Back in the 1860s, most Americans earnestly desired the construction of a transcontinental railroad to unite the Atlantic and Pacific coasts. Two railroad companies, the Central Pacific and the Union Pacific, were attempting to build such a line, but they were having serious problems, and many people doubted they would succeed.

Therefore, as a kind of insurance, Congress authorized the construction of an alternate transcontinental railroad in 1866. This new line, which was to extend from Springfield, Missouri, to the Pacific, would be built by the Atlantic and Pacific Railroad (A&P). At the same time, Congress authorized an upstart California concern known as the Southern Pacific Railroad (SP) to build a line south from San Francisco to connect with the proposed new A&P railroad.

Planning roughly to follow the 35th Parallel west to the coast, the A&P carried out surveys and started construction near St. Louis, Missouri. After the track had been laid 327 miles into Indian Territory, the A&P went broke. Reorganized as a subsidiary of the St. Louis and San Francisco Railway Company, commonly called Frisco, it still lacked funds for such an enormous construction project.

To the rescue came a vigorous Atchison, Topeka & Santa Fe Railroad (Santa Fe). Having started in 1859 as the Atchison and Topeka Railroad, after connecting those two towns, it added Santa Fe to its name and continued to expand westward. By 1879 when it began negotiating with the Frisco, it wanted to control a line all the way to the Pacific. Consequently, a few months later, the A&P was ready to go again, now under the joint direction of the Santa Fe and the Frisco.

As the A&P built into Arizona, its potential competition in California in the form of the Southern Pacific became quite concerned. The SP had taken over the Central Pacific Railroad, thus acquiring part of the original transcontinental railroad which had been completed in 1869. It had also built south to Mojave, Los Angeles, and Yuma, Arizona. Then, pushing eastward, it built across Arizona and New Mexico, and into Texas where it connected with the Texas and Pacific Railroad. The SP thus gained control over the second transcontinental railroad into California. But the A&P threatened to end the SP's monopoly.

To the directors of the SP, such a loss seemed intolerable. So they set out to gain control over what was expected to become the third transcontinental line to California. They could not take over the A&P because the Santa Fe and Frisco each owned one-half of its outstanding stock. Instead they purchased sufficient Frisco stock to gain two seats on the Board of Directors. As a result, early in 1882 the Frisco developed a rather sudden inability to continue financing its share of the construction of the A&P.

But the Santa Fe did what it could, and the A&P was completed as far as the east bank of the Colorado River in May 1883. An A&P work crew then went across the river to complete track to Needles, which, as will be noted shortly, had already been reached by the Southern

Pacific a month earlier.

What remained was the construction of a major bridge across the Colorado, but this seemingly ordinary assignment proved to be extremely difficult. Time and again newly driven pilings would be washed out only a few hours later. While quicksand and high water were the principal culprits, other problems included a wrecked pile-driving barge and an entire dormitory train burned down by a drunken cook. The bridge was finally finished early in August, although, as a result of flooding and ever heavier traffic, it had to be relocated and to be rebuilt several times.

The "Thirty-fifth Parallel Trans-Continental Line" was officially opened to traffic on August 9, 1883. Passengers and freight would ride the A&P to Needles, where they would transfer to the SP. The Santa Fe-controlled A&P would continue construction westward from Needles when and if sufficient funds became available.

Meanwhile, having caused a major delay in the construction of the proposed A&P transcontinental line by placing its own people on the Frisco's Board of Directors, the SP took advantage of the situation with a vigorous construction program of its own. It sent out two crews to survey a route from Mojave, 239 miles to Needles. One pushed eastward from Mojave. The other, after traveling up the Colorado from Yuma by steamboat, thrust westward from Needles. Once the route had been determined, construction got under way in Mojave in early February 1882.

Laying track at the rate of approximately ten miles per month, by late October the railroad reached Waterman's, the site of an ore crushing mill on the north bank of the Mojave River about a mile west of what was to become Barstow.

Facilitated by advance crews strung along the projected road, track layers speeded up production to just over one mile per day during November and December. Thus, by the end of 1882, the SP's new line had extended beyond Calico Station -- a few months later renamed Daggett -- and Ludlow almost to Bagdad. Using principally Chinese labor, a total of 131 miles of railroad had been completed.

At the one-year mark, February 1883, tracks were approaching Amboy, and someone conceived the idea of naming the succeeding sidings and stations alphabetically. So, following Amboy, they were named Bristol, Cadiz, Danby, Edson, Fenner, Goffs, Homer, Ibex, and Java. Later on, Bristol became Bengal, and Edson became Essex. While such changes did not upset the carefully planned alphabetical order, subsequent construction of additional sidings and the temporary renaming of Goffs -- it was called Blake for a time -- certainly did.

The SP's line was completed to Needles on April 19, 1883, fully a month before A&P rails reached the Colorado from the East. Thus the directors of the SP appeared to have accomplished what they had set out to do -- to prevent the A&P from completing a third transcontinental railroad through California to the Pacific.

It was an accomplishment bought at a fairly high price, though. The Mojave Desert provided the SP with very little revenue -- not enough even to make operating expenses. Between Mojave and Ludlow, for example, there was only one station -- at Daggett. Daggett also had a roundhouse. While there were no fewer than six other carded stops between those two places, they did not amount to much -- aside from the required water tanks, there was a sum total of two buildings: a section house and a tool shed at Waterman. That was it for 124 miles of the western half of the SP's Colorado Division. The eastern half, from Daggett to Needles was even more barren, though perhaps more business could be expected from that area because of its working mines, such as the Bonanza King, which was then being touted as the richest silver mine in California. Unfortunately for all concerned, most of the mines proved to be unproductive, with even the Bonanza King closing down after a mill fire in 1885.

If, in keeping with the Santa Fe's transcontinental ambitions, the A&P wished to continue to the coast, it would have to build parallel to the SP. But to construct another railway across the Mojave Desert to compete for business that was far from sufficient to support a single line did not make economic sense -- especially when the A&P was already struggling just to stay afloat.

Of course, there was an alternative. The A&P might arrange to purchase SP line from Needles to Mojave, or even beyond, and then acquire running rights over SP lines to Oakland or San Francisco. Thus the Santa Fe would have its transcontinental route.

But negotiations with the SP got nowhere at all because the reason for building its Colorado Division from Mojave to Needles in the first place had been to prevent the A&P from gaining access to the Pacific coast. As SP officials saw it, they had accomplished what they had set out to do. The A&P had nothing more than a very long branch line through sparsely populated territory to Needles, and if that caused the A&P to go bankrupt, certainly it was none of SP's concern. In fact, SP people were quite smugly satisfied about the entire matter. They fully expected the A&P to give up.

Affairs might have turned out as the SP expected had it not been for the Santa Fe. The Santa Fe had a lot of funds invested in the A&P, and it had no intention of losing them. Moreover, it intended to gain access to the Pacific coast. The Santa Fe, therefore, started making surveys for an extension of the A&P line that would parallel the SP's. Furthermore, it let it be known that it planned construction.

Now it was the SP's turn to be worried. If the Santa Fe did as it was threatening to do, it would be the SP, not the A&P, that would be stuck with a long and unprofitable stretch of track in the desert.

Negotiations got under way again, and this time an agreement was reached. Its terms called for the A&P to purchase the SP's Colorado Division as soon as the seller could provide clear title. Because the clearing of the title might require some time, the A&P would lease the line from the SP until then. Moreover, the A&P managed to secure an option for trackage rights over the SP line from Mojave to Oakland and San Francisco, and the use of SP's terminals at both ports. This agreement, constituting four separate contracts, went into effect on October 1, 1884.

A year later, as a result of additional negotiating and financing on the part of its parent, the Santa Fe, the A&P acquired access from Barstow, over Cajon Pass to San Diego and Los Angeles. Thus the Santa Fe succeeded in becoming a true transcontinental railroad to the Pacific, and it broke the SP's monopoly as well.

As a consequence of financial problems and reorganizations involving all three corporations involved in the operation of this transcontinental route -- the Santa

Fe, the St. Louis & San Francisco (Frisco), and the A&P -- the Santa Fe came to control most of the line. In fact, the A&P ceased to exist in 1897. But it was not until 1911 that the Santa Fe acquired title to the SP track between Needles and Mojave, by giving its line from Benson, Arizona, to Guaymas, Mexico, plus some cash, in exchange.

One holdover from the days of the SP in the Mojave is the land that was granted to it by the United States Government as an inducement for building a railroad through largely uninhabited territory. Aside from the right-of-way and other railroad related lands sold to the Santa Fe, the SP kept its land. As a result, as recently as 1980 it still owned well over 800,000 acres scattered in separate parcels, checker-board fashion, throughout the desert. Most of it adjoined BLM-managed land. Because their goals differ, this pattern of ownership made it difficult for both the SP and the BLM to manage their holdings effectively. Therefore, as a consequence of the California Desert Conservation Area (CDCA) plan of 1980, the Southern Pacific Land Company, which manages SP lands, and the BLM got together to attempt to arrange mutually agreeable exchanges based on the concept of value for value. During the next three years of negotiations the federal government acquired title to some 100,000 acres of SP land in exchange for property located mainly in northern California. These exchanges, although mutually advantageous ground to a halt when the SP became involved in merger efforts with the Santa Fe and other railroads. Now that the Denver and Rio Grande appears to be in control of the SP, the program of exchanges is expected to resume.

By the beginning of this century it was obvious

that what had been the SP's failure to prevent railroad competition in California had succeeded in opening the Mojave Desert to various types of development, especially mining. Other railroads were soon built to connect with this transcontinental source and outlet.

The first was a short, mile-long spur built by Frank Monaghan and Dan Murphy to facilitate transportation of merchandise to and from their store in Needles and boats tied up on the bank of the Colorado River. Because it was so short and there was a minimum of traffic, the rolling stock of this railroad consisted of a few handcars. Motive force consisted of a number of Indians hired to push and pull the handcars as needed. In time, therefore, this spur came to be known as the "M&M Pushcar Line."

Other East Mojave railroads that connected with the Needles-Mojave line were more significant -- some considerably so. The subject of separate treatment elsewhere in the Guide to the East Mojave Heritage Trail, the most important were the Nevada Southern Railway extending north from Goffs (Vol. I, pp. 145-150), and the Tonopah and Tidewater Railroad running north from Ludlow (Vol. II, pp. 132-149). Both were standard-gauge lines. So also was the much less significant Ludlow & Southern Railway extending some eight miles south from Ludlow to the Bagdad-Chase mines at Steadman. Built in 1903, it stopped regular service in 1916 and was taken up in 1935.

Two narrow-gauge railroads serving mining interests on Bristol Lake also reached the Santa Fe's Needles-Barstow line. The first, generally termed the "gypsum railroad," served gypsum quarries south of Amboy from about 1905 to 1924. The second extended from Saltus, on the Santa Fe just east of Amboy, a few miles south onto the generally dry bed of Bristol Lake where salt was mined. Although the mining of salt continues, the railroad, started about 1911, was taken up in 1976.

Two additional narrow-gauge railroads reached the AT&SF main line at Daggett. The first was generally called the Calico Railroad. Built in 1888, it served Calico, Daggett, and several different mines. Much of it was taken up in 1903, but it was not fully dismantled until 1907. The second, the Borate and Daggett, was built in 1898 to serve borate mines in the Calico Mountains. Eleven miles long, the Borate and Daggett was quite active for several years. It was taken up after the Pacific Coast Borax Company shifted its mining operations to the Death Valley area in 1907.

The Santa Fe itself built an extension from central Arizona to Cadiz. Starting on the outskirts of Phoenix in 1905, the branch finally reached the main line at Cadiz in 1910. Unlike the other branch railroads, this one is still actively in business.

Each addition brought more traffic, both passengers and freight. Within only a relatively few years, especially considering that this was a line through sparsely populated desert, the capacity of its single track was being severely tested, and a second track became desirable. It was built piecemeal over the years, with full double-track operation between Needles and Barstow becoming a reality in 1923.

The railroad helped populate several areas of the East Mojave by providing water from its springs and wells at Newberry -- at a cost of two cents per gallon in 1885. Today, places such as Ludlow and Amboy still

233.

receive their water supply by train. And despite more than a century of inflation, the AT&SF charges less for it today than it did back in 1885 -- at approximately $134 per full 16,000-gallon tank car, less than one cent per gallon.

Years ago far more places used Santa Fe water, but with dieselization ending the requirement of water tanks every few miles, even busy little towns like Bagdad -- once a mining center and an important helper station located at the foot of Ash Hill and the 1.44% grade to Squaw Summit -- were eventually entirely abandoned. Fortunately for the Santa Fe, the decline in local traffic that naturally followed has been made up, and more, by increased interstate traffic over the years.

The two most important East Mojave Desert places served by the Santa Fe were Needles and Barstow. Needles, of course, became important as soon as the SP and the A&P built their separate lines into town. As the eastern terminus of its Colorado Division from Mojave, the SP found it necessary to build reasonably extensive facilities in Needles, including a station large enough to accommodate 500 people, a hotel, and a fourteen-stall roundhouse. The A&P built several structures, also, but they were not so extensive. Later, after the AT&SF took over, all the facilities were greatly expanded. By 1920 more than 1,200 residents of Needles were working for the Santa Fe.

Barstow, located on the south bank of the Mojave River, just across from Waterman's, also became important because of the railroad. Named for Santa Fe President William Barstow Strong, it developed into the northern terminus for the company's roads in southern California and the southern terminus for its lines into the central and northern part of the state. The railroad maintains a large classification yard and major service facilities there.

While the story of the Santa Fe in the East Mojave is replete with tales of runaway trains, accidents, and even pursuit of trains by a ghost, probably the most famous event was its hosting of the Coyote Special in 1905. Walter Scott, a prospector better known today as Death Valley Scotty, wandered into Barstow on a particularly hot early summer day in 1905. Barstow seemed to have little to offer Scotty that day, aside from a place to put up his mules and the train station. He was on his way to Los Angeles, and he wanted to get there yesterday. But when he arrived at the station he discovered that not only was the day a scorcher, there was no train leaving for Los Angeles any time soon.

Scotty was nothing if not resourceful. Could he have a charter train? Yes he could. And a short while later he was on his way to Los Angeles in his own special train. Chartering a train was not something commonly done, so it was only natural that reporters should be waiting for him at his destination. Scotty regaled them with stories of his trip, then delightedly read the ensuing publicity.

If chartering a train to take him from Barstow to Los Angeles could make him a local celebrity, what might a longer trip accomplish? What if he could also establish a speed record? There was only one way to find out. So Scotty hied himself to the Santa Fe office in Los Angeles and asked if the railroad would be willing to transport him and his party from Los Angeles to Chicago in 46 hours or less. The fee settled upon was $5,500.

The Coyote Special, as his train was called, left

Los Angeles on Sunday, July 9, 1905. With speeds of up to 106 miles per hour and with only a relatively few stops to swap locomotives, to take on supplies, and to provide the newspapers with plenty of copy, the Coyote Special roared across the East Mojave and on to the midwest, arriving in Chicago ahead of schedule 44 hours and 54 minutes later.

The stunt was a smashing success. Scotty became a national celebrity and the Santa Fe held a speed record that was to stand for nearly thirty years.

Even more famous than the Coyote Special were some of the Santa Fe's name trains that carried people from Los Angeles, across the East Mojave, to points east such as Kansas City or Chicago. The first of these famous trains was the California Limited. Started in 1892, by 1903 it made the Los Angeles-Chicago trip in 69 hours. Operating almost continuously for the next fifty years, and offering free roses for the ladies and cuisine by Fred Harvey, it was extremely popular. On one memorable occasion it operated in 23 sections westbound and 22 sections eastbound -- all in the same day. Other well known AT&SF name trains include the Los Angeles Express, the Missionary, the Chicago Flyer, and the Grand Canyon Limited. The first all-diesel name train on the Santa Fe was the Super Chief which, starting in 1936, operated between Los Angeles and Chicago on a schedule of just under 40 hours.

Although the Santa Fe continued to purchase steam locomotives through the year 1944, by 1940 it knew that the locomotive of the future was the diesel. Diesels offered a number of ways of saving money, especially when operated in multiple units: they could be handled by smaller crews, they could be repaired on the road, and they required fewer helpers on the grades. Additionally, they could go much farther than steam locomotives between servicings. For example, fifteen stops to change steam locomotives were commonly required on the Los Angeles-Chicago run alone. Diesel power could handle the entire distance without major servicing. In the desert, though, the most significant economy offered by the diesels was their ability to pass up water stops. As a result, complete dieselization was accomplished in 1954.

Today, the Santa Fe line through the East Mojave Desert is an integral component of a thoroughly modern rail system. With 11,700 miles of track extending from Chicago to San Francisco and from Galveston to San Diego, it ranks seventh nationwide.

INTRODUCTION TO THE GEOLOGY
of the FOURTH SEGMENT of the
EAST MOJAVE HERITAGE TRAIL

by Steven Pencall

To try to sum up the geology of a region as vast as that encompassed by the Fourth Segment in a few words is to risk gross injustice both to the reader and to the rocks. However, as you will soon see, there are unifying themes that help make a jumble of rocks comprehensible. These themes are volcanism, tectonism (earth movements), and weathering in an arid climate.

Even a casual traveler passing over the Fourth Segment is impressed by the abundance and variety of volcanic rocks seen along the Trail. Virtually every common type of volcanic rock and some less common types as well, are represented somewhere along the Trail.

Volcanic rocks are divided into four broad groups based on the amount of silica (quartz) that they contain. In order of increasing silica content, they are classified as basalts, andesites, dacites, and rhyolites. Although it is not an infallible guide, they generally become lighter in color as silica content increases. It is possible to find all of these types of rocks along the Fourth Segment although dacites, rhyolites, and their close relatives, the latites, predominate.

It is worth bearing in mind however, that a cursory examination of a geologic map of the region reveals that volcanic rocks are a minority of rocks in the area. Metamorphic rocks, those which were formed from other rocks that have undergone change as a result of heat and pressure, are actually exposed over the largest area. Also widespread in the area are plutonic rocks which were molten masses that cooled deep in the crust.

It is also apparent that volcanism in the area traversed by the Fourth Segment is long dead. There are no cinder cones or jagged lava flows to suggest the landscape of ancient times. Nearly all of these volcanic rocks were formed in the interval from 14 to 27 million years ago. Even neglecting the volume of rock already lost to erosion, this indicates a period, brief in geologic terms, of intense volcanism. One common type of rock along the Fourth Segment is ignimbrite, or welded tuff, formed as a brief violent eruption spewed a cloud of red-hot ash and pumice that fused into a solid mass upon settling to the ground. Such eruptions could easily incinerate all living things for many miles around.

Occurring more or less simultaneously with the volcanism, and related to it, was a still incompletely understood process geologists call detachment faulting. This is not the type of faulting exemplified by the San Andreas Fault and other notorious faults where sections of the Earth's crust move sideways past one another along an approximately vertical plane. Rather, it is akin to a giant landslide, where huge sections of the crust, many square miles in extent, broke loose along fractures several miles deep in the crust and slid down gently sloping ramps in response to gravity. It is believed that the Earth's crust in this region began to stretch and become thinner about 35 million years ago. As it became thinner, more heat flowed from the interior of the Earth. This heat caused the crust to warp into a series of very broad arches and troughs. In simplest terms, the uppermost crust on the arches broke loose and slid into the troughs.

This phenomenon was unknown in the Mojave

Desert prior to 1960 and its significance and extent were not fully realized until the early 1980s. It is now known that a huge area of southeastern California, southern Nevada, and western Arizona, an area of tens of thousands of square miles, has undergone detachment faulting.

Those parts of the mountain ranges in the area which are in the detached, or upper plate, are now resting on top of rocks to which they are completely unrelated. This discovery has profound implications for the geology of western North America and has stimulated intense interest in the area from geologists and other earth scientists. It is quite possible that you may encounter scientists doing field work in this area.

Finally, all of these Earth materials and processes have occurred in a region which now has a very arid climate. Much of what little rain does fall occurs in brief, intense storms that wash away rock debris that would form soil. With little soil and vegetation to soften their profile, the mountains take on their familiar jagged appearance. The lack of soil and vegetation makes the process of observing and interpreting the geology much easier.

EAST MOJAVE WILDLIFE
by Mike McGill

Each year more and more people flock to the East Mojave to spend a few days of peaceful solitude. They come for a variety of reasons, but many, if not most, have an interest in the wildlife that visits their camp. Desert animals are very interesting; they have to endure cold, blustery winds, little moisture, and, of course, high temperatures.

In these days of rapid development, overpopulation, and environmental pollution, much of our wildlife is threatened or endangered in one way or another. To have some idea of conditions wildlife in the desert must cope with daily, you have to know first what constitutes a desert. Everyone has their own definition, but one way or another a lack of rainfall would be included. Historically, people considered low average precipitation in a given area, usually less than ten inches annually, all that was needed for the definition. Today, the evaporation rate has to be taken into consideration. No matter how much rain falls in an area, if there is more evaporation than rain, it will be dry.

If an animal loses more water to evaporation, either through sweating or panting, than it takes in eating or drinking, then it will dehydrate and die. The causes of evaporation are complicated, but high radiation (sunshine), high winds, and high temperatures are all contributors. One of the reasons you feel relatively cooler in the deserts at high temperatures and low humidities is that your perspiration evaporates rapidly. If the area receives less than ten inches of rain per year, and the evaporation rate exceeds ten inches per year, a desert will be formed, whether it is hot or cold, sandy or not!

But animals do live in the desert. A walk at night with a flashlight or a little patience during the daytime will reveal a variety of mammals, reptiles, amphibians, birds, and insects. Notice that when we speak of "animals or wildlife" of the desert, all the above categories apply. The desert is not a barren, desolate place as many people would have us believe; there is a great diversity of wildlife here.

In simple terms, there are basically three ways in which animals can arrange their lives in the hot East Mojave: evade the heat, passively put up with it, or combat it by the cooling evaporation of water.

We will briefly examine these possibilities. The simplest way to evade the heat is to go underground. A few inches down the tremendous temperature variations are smoothed out, and the temperature does not reach the extremes of the soil surface and the atmosphere. The burrowing animals, mainly rodents, can come out in the cool night and lead a normal, but nocturnal, life.

Putting up with the heat by remaining on the surface during the day would, unless water is evaporated, inevitably cause the body temperature to rise. This would necessitate an increased tolerance to high body temperature beyond the limit found in other animals. But there is no evidence to the fact that any desert animal has a temperature tolerance much higher than its relative in a more moderate climate. Knowledge is limited in this area. Much more research is needed. If there is one animal that can tolerate the heat, it would be the insect. As all of us have seen during the hottest part of the day, insects can be seen either flying around our head or crawling up the side of a hot barren sand dune.

Fighting the heat by evaporation is efficient, but expensive in an environment where little or no water is available. Where no open water is available, animals can still use the water contained in plants or the bodies of their prey. An increased need for water to combat the heat emphasizes the extreme dryness of the desert and the scarcity of water. The large animals have no chance of hiding underground during the day; at best they can rest in the little shade they may find. Therefore, these animals are faced with the dilemma of spending their scant water resources for evaporation or virtually being cooked!

This brings us to the two important subjects of water and temperature regulation. Mainly we will be concerned with mammals. Water regulation is maintaining proper fluid balance in the body. This is especially difficult for land dwelling organisms. There are a number of ways in which a mammal can lose water: urine/feces, evaporative cooling, respiration, or, in the case of females, lactation. But to counteract these losses, especially in desert animals, the efficiency of the kidneys is very good and therefore makes the animal more efficient at combating this loss.

To live in the East Mojave, animals have processes which can be classified into behavioral and physiological. Behavioral can be, simply, avoidance. Physiological would be the existence of mechanisms for obtaining water more efficiently and not losing water so quickly. The white-throated wood rat *(Neotoma ambigula)* commonly found in the East Mojave is a good behaviorial example. His den can be seen as a huge pile of sticks among the boulders or under a tree. The air temperature in the area may be 125 degrees, but inside, under the pile of sticks, it will be a "cool" 105 degrees. Also inside this pile, the rat digs a shallow depression in the ground; this further takes the temperature down to around 95 degrees.

Neotoma gets around rapid water loss by: 1. Taking in as much water as possible by eating cacti. 2. Using a seasonal dietary shift, in the spring eating succulent plants and in the summer switching to insects. 3. Using the water in the plants. Although the plants are high in salt, *Neotoma* can take out the salt with its highly efficient kidneys. Some other rodents can deal with a salt concentration two to three times as salty as sea water!

There are other methods used by animals to cope with water loss. They may be a periodic drinker and take in large quantities of water at any given time and use this water over the drier spells. An excellent example of this is the desert bighorn which can go a week without taking on water and then rehydrate the body completely at one drink. A human cannot do this; no matter how thirsty, he cannot rehydrate his body all at once. A human drinks his fill, waits 15 or 20 minutes and drinks again until full, waits another 15 or 20 minutes and drinks again, etc., until his body is rehydrated. Obviously, a human in the desert, no matter how much he drinks, gradually becomes dehydrated. The desert bighorn can lose up to 30% of its body weight, mostly water, before it dies; a human only 10 to 15%.

An animal does not want to lose its water in the circulatory system. In the circulatory system the blood must be kept liquid enough and flowing through the system to cool the brain. When humans begin dying from dehydration, the mind is the first thing that goes. The brain is not kept cool enough. The blood gets thicker and cannot flow to the brain to cool it.

Using the bighorn example again, when it has lost

30% of its body weight, only 10% of the fluid is from the circulatory system. Humans lose water evenly throughout the body, therefore, our cooling system breaks down before that of the desert bighorn.

Evaporative cooling is the primary mechanism for heat dissipation for desert ungulates (hoofed animals). This includes panting and sweating with panting being more efficient. Desert bighorn and cattle use these methods with cattle sweating and bighorn doing both. Keep in mind that evaporation accounts for the major expenditure of water in animals in the East Mojave. The desert bighorns seek shade, higher elevations, cool soil or rocks, and breezes that cool. Cooling appears to be achieved mainly by evaporation and by direct contact to cooler rocks and ground.

Briefly, two other means of coping with water regulation exist: going into torpor and oxidizing of food for water. Torpor is simply slowing down the heart rate and metabolic activity so low that an animal is sluggish or dormant. This is very temporary. A hummingbird does this every night. An animal is helpless while in torpor, but comes out of it quickly.

Oxidizing of food involves metabolizing carbohydrates (food) and extracting the water. In other words, the animal never has to take a drink of standing water. The kangaroo rat is a good example. Another fascinating fact about the kangaroo rat: its urine has five times the concentration of dissolved salts and other minerals in it than humans which is two times as concentrated as sea water. Theoretically a kangaroo rat could drink sea water and survive! There are many more complex systems for water regulation, but the ones presented here show how critical water and water regulation are for animals in a desert environment.

Temperature regulation is the animal's ability to withstand temperature extremes. Temperature regulation has allowed mammals to be decoupled from their environment more so than other vertebrates and live in areas of much greater extremes of temperature than most other organisms. Biologists say that an animal can be endothermic or ectothermic. An endothermic (mammals and birds) animal is one whose body temperature is controlled largely by metabolic activity and by precise regulation of heat exchange with the environment. Ectothermic (cold blooded), on the other hand, is when the body temperature is regulated largely by heat gained from the surroundings rather than by metabolic heat (reptiles). Most animals are ectothermic. Most endothermic animals maintain a high and fairly constant body temperature throughout life, but for this they pay an extremely high cost in energy.

Under optimum temperature conditions, a mammal expends five to ten times more energy for maintenance than a reptile of equal size and equal body temperature. At lower temperatures, the cost of maintaining a high body temperature rises abruptly: a mammal uses 33 times more energy than a reptile at 68 degrees and 100 times more at 50 degrees. A foraging mouse uses 20 to 30 times more energy than a foraging lizard of equal weight. In small mammals, such as most rodents, 80 to 90 per cent of the total energy budget goes for thermoregulation. The costs of endothermy are clearly high. Many benefits exist though: mammals and birds can be active under an array of temperature extremes; they are freed from dependence on the sunlit part of the daily light-dark cycle and from becoming inactive during cold seasons (active through all seasons and being nocturnal). Finally, maximum oxygen transport capability and high rates of enzyme action are supported by high body temperatures. All of these greatly enhance the ability of the animal to sustain high levels of activity.

The normal range of body temperature for a mammal is 86 to 110 degrees Fahrenheit. Air temperatures range from 122 degrees to lower than -58 degrees Fahrenheit. Their body temperature upper limit is around 112 degrees; lower limit around freezing. How do animals deal with these extremes? They either go into torpor or have daily cycles. The temperature cheapest for animals to operate in is called the Thermal Neutral Zone (TNZ). It is the region where it is metabolically cheapest for the animal to live or operate in. On either side, for example, humans will shiver or sweat. An animal can expand this TNZ by decreasing his thermal conductance - - this is the temperature gradient between the body core temperature and the air temperature. The higher the gradient the more likely the body will give off or take on heat. The animal tries to insulate himself from the environment using hair or feathers.

Mammalian heat stress in the East Mojave can be difficult to cope with. How do they deal with it? Normally, avoidance is the answer. This is related to the size of the animal. Smaller animals have a higher surface to volume ratio -- they take on or give off heat more quickly than a larger animal. A skinny person will cool off or heat up more quickly than a fatter person. Of course, an animal can dig burrows or build a nest like the white-throated wood rat discussed earlier. A jackrabbit has its large ears to help regulate body temperatures; in the still shade during the day the blood vessels in the jackrabbit's ears vasodilate -- become larger, more blood goes through them; on a windy day, it doesn't want to lose water so the blood vessels vasoconstrict -- become smaller in diameter. So the jackrabbit's ears behave like a living radiator! A smaller animal, like a rodent, uses various behavior patterns. All of us have seen the tiny ground squirrels scampering around seemingly at all hours of the day. On the desert we see two types. From daylight to around ten o'clock in the morning and during the late afternoon until dark, the round-tailed ground squirrel is out -- simply avoiding the extreme temperatures during the day in its burrow; during the hottest part of the day we see the antelope ground squirrel. It has white stripes along its body and carries its tail over its back while running. This animal handles the high temperature in a variety of ways. Its metabolic rate is lower than expected for its size. This allows them to preserve water while in their burrows. Most other rodents are similar. But besides a lower metabolic rate, the antelope ground squirrel can increase its thermal conductance, thereby dumping heat into the environment. They also produce less heat. The squirrel's thermal neutral zone is from 95 to 106 degrees. It will run into its cooler burrow to dump heat, then go out again and take up more heat. It can also go into volunteer hyperthermia to lose heat or salivate on itself to keep cooler by evaporative cooling. Voluntary hyperthermia is allowing the body temperature to go above the air temperature. At other times they urinate on themselves to keep cooler (some bats do this also).

Volunteer hyperthermia is more common in large animals than in smaller ones because smaller animals have higher surface to volume ratios and can dump heat into the environment more quickly or take on heat more quickly. A large animal takes on heat more slowly so it can stay out longer. Animals also use a complex system called the counter-current system to keep their brain cool. This involves the nasal passages and specific circulatory tissues. It is much too complex to go into here, but this system is more important to a large animal living in the open, such as some carnivores.

As can be seen, wildlife in the East Mojave have complicated physical and behavioral systems that play an important role in their existence. Hopefully now when encountering the animals in our desert you can appreciate them a little more. Enjoy the wildlife, but, on the other hand, try not to cause them undue stress; they have enough already!

COYOTE

Anyone who has spent time in the desert has seen the coyote many times. A coyote, also called a brush wolf or gray wolf, is a typical wild dog. They are the largest carnivorous animal regularly found in the desert. Being that it is so common and large is an attribute to its cunning and skill because large animals are usually the first to go when man comes on the scene. Coyotes are one of the best runners among the canids with average speeds around 25 to 30 miles per hour with top speeds at around 40 miles per hour. They have also been known to travel great distances, up to 400 miles over a period of time. Unlike the wolf, which runs with its tail horizontal, a coyote runs with its tail down. Coyotes are very territorial.

As all members of the family *Canidae,* the coyote has five toes on each front foot and four on each hind

Long-legged, lean, and mean, the coyote
can be found anywhere in the East Mojave.
Generally they are not a threat to humans,
<u>if</u> you leave them alone.

4 October 1981
Dennis Casebier Photo

foot. Their tracks are nearly in a straight line. The gestation period can be as short as seven weeks or as long as nine weeks. The young, usually five to seven, are born in a hollow log, den, or burrow. The coyote's life span is from 10 to 15 years. The male and female are seen together and both share in rearing the pups; both feed the pups, the mother with her milk and the father through regurgitation of his stomach contents. After about six weeks the pups begin hunting with the adults, thereby learning techniques that will enable them to survive on their own.

A fully grown coyote can weigh up to 50 pounds, but they are usually smaller. Coyotes are basically lazy and will tend to travel on previously used trails, roads, or paths with their scat being seen there or on a hill, open spot, or on a vantage point where they watch for prey.

The coyote is an omnivore. This means they eat almost anything. They feed extensively on plant material with one study revealing that up to 40% of a coyote's diet was made up of vegetable matter. Such things as seeds, grasses, fruit, and flowers are eaten regularly. Of course, meat is taken with rabbits, ground squirrels, and kangaroo rats making up most of this diet. Coyotes are also known to eat scorpions, spiders, and other insects.

A coyote is more often heard than seen, being mainly nocturnal and only occasionally being seen during the day. Regardless of what the western movies tell you, a coyote's howl is infrequent. Vocalizations are varied with most of them heard at dawn, dusk, or during the night and consisting of a series of short "yips" or barks followed by the infrequent howl. A chorus with several other coyotes in not uncommon.

The coyote has been relentlessly trapped as well as

shot by mindless gunners. Also ill-advised poisoning campaigns have robbed much of the West of the chorus of the coyote. With this removal, there has been an increase of rodents which, in turn, leads to the demands for more poisoning, trapping, or shooting. When will we learn the danger of indiscriminate destruction of a species?

JACKRABBIT

Even if you are an infrequent visitor to the East Mojave you will probably have seen a large animal with long ears bounding away from you. More than likely it was the black-tailed jackrabbit, but on occasion an antelope jackrabbit is spotted. Basically the only difference is the black-tailed has black on the surface of the tail and on the tips of the ears, whereas the antelope does not. The antelope is also larger.

Of course the jackrabbit is not a rabbit at all, it is a hare. Its young are fully furred, with eyes open, and mobile almost immediately upon birth. The mother takes care of the young for only about a month before they are on their own. Jackrabbits never go underground, but instead make a stomped out, shallow depression in the grass under a bush or tree, called a "form," where the three or four young are born. Only one percent live to see their second year.

Generally speaking a jackrabbit is defenseless against its predators except for its speed, which can be as high as 35 mph. But anyone who has ever been kicked by a jackrabbit knows that this is not necessarily so -- those large and powerful hind feet can make you well aware of how powerful they really are. The bucks (males) use them to fight with. They also have very good eyesight and hearing.

The jackrabbit is well suited for the desert. He has a long lean body, large hind legs, and large feet, a small head, in proportion to the body size, and, of course, those large ears protruding from it. He will weigh up to ten pounds.

TED JENSEN

The jackrabbit must have water. It does not necessarily have to be water as we know it. It can be water locked up in green leaves or perennial plants that spring up after a rain, mesquite, and grass shoots. They are browsers and have sharp edged teeth all around. In the winter, the jackrabbit depends on woody and dried vegetation. They feed primarily early in the morning for an hour or so and in the evenings, sometimes feeding after dark.

The jackrabbit keeps cool by radiating heat from its large ears and by sitting in a depression under the shade of a bush or tree. It also pants, but not typical panting such as found in a dog. Also, remarkably, he will lose water from his surface by evaporation -- very costly, even though they have no sweat glands. This is called cutaneous evaporation or insensible perspiration. These methods seem to be the only way that a non-burrowing, medium-sized animal can survive without large amounts of drinking water in a hot desert.

A person can sometimes walk up to jackrabbits without them moving. This is quite common if it has not been shot at. Jackrabbits know that humans are no threat to them, so to conserve energy and water, they stay sitting under a bush in the shade. Obviously, jackrabbits and other wildlife, when being pursued by dogs or shot at continuously, will not allow a person to approach them.

Jackrabbits do some damage to crops and become a problem due to the senseless killing of its natural enemies. Recently jackrabbits have become uncommon in some areas because of road kills and destruction of habitat, as well as hunting. Even so, the jackrabbit is widespread and abundant in most areas.

HARVESTER ANTS

All of us while in the East Mojave have seen the large crater-like nests along the trail or roadside. These are the nests of harvester ants. The two genera that inhabit these craters are *Pogonomyrmex* and *Veromessor*. If the ant is all black, they are the *Veromessor;* if they are all black, but with a reddish abdomen, these are the *Pogonomyrmex*. The *Veromessors* are found in great abundance particularly north of the Santa Fe Railway. One species of *Pogonomyrmex,* the bearded harvester, has special combs on its forelegs used to remove the accumulation of dust and sand from its body; these in turn are cleaned by passing them through basket-like "beards" of long hairs on the under surface of the head.

Harvester ant craters sometimes measure two feet across and are the result of the movement of debris, plant material, or dead ants, from their underground chambers to the area next to the nest opening. Most of the debris is discarded seed husks, lightweight, and blows away easily. The worker ants and wingless sterile females can carry loads in excess of ten times their body weight -- a human weightlifter cannot come close to this feat.

Ants are ectothermic -- cold blooded. On cold, cloudy days they move in slow motion; on warm days they move around quickly; but on very hot days they go underground to escape the intense heat.

Seeds make up the staple food supply of the colony. They are cut up and the starchy material removed by their tongues. The seeds are gathered in excess and stored for later use. The annual crop of seeds each summer is short in duration but the harvesters have adapted to this cycle and survive the other months from this storage. The harvesters are also very territorial and will defend their home against unwelcome intruders, including stray workers from other colonies, which may end up as food.

The work that goes on in the harvesting above ground and in the underground chambers is endless. There are three castes within the colony: queens, workers, and males. The queens are large, start the colony, and are an egg-laying machine. The males are wingless, smaller than queens and are short-lived, dying after mating. Occasionally workers may lay eggs.

The tireless efforts of the harvesters may give us a feeling of guilt -- rarely do we yield such productivity! Normally, the various species in these two genera go unnoticed. Beware, the members of the genus *Pogonomyrmex* produce a painful sting.

SIDEWINDER

There are many types of rattlesnakes in the desert, including the western diamondback, red diamondback, Mitchell's or speckled, and the Mojave Green, but there is only one that is specially adapted to the desert environment -- the sidewinder.

It comes complete with sun shields, a good sense of temperature regulation, and a peculiar mode of travel for operating in sandy areas. Also called the horned rattler or little horned rattler, it gets its name from its sideways locomotion and its characteristic horns which are sharp scales above the eyes. The body moves in an S-shaped curve and leaves behind a series of J-shaped tracks in the loose sand. The J-end points in the direction of travel. The sidewinder is the smallest of our rattlesnakes reaching only from one to two-and-one-half feet in length.

Do not let its small size fool you. This snake is both dangerous and aggressive and has a bad temper. They resent being kicked or stepped on! People have reported being chased by them! The sidewinder is a rattlesnake and therefore is poisonous with deaths having been reported from their bite. Being a nocturnal animal, it needs more than poison to obtain its food of lizards, mice, and other small mammals. Located on either side of

Rattlesnakes, like this sidewinder, are an integral part of the ecology of the desert. They are extremely dangerous. Give them a wide berth.
The best cure for snake bite is to avoid being bitten.

Dennis Casebier Photo

their face are two pits which are heat sensitive. These sensors tell them exactly where to strike when pursuing warm-blooded prey.

Sidewinders are found from below sea level to about 5,000 feet usually in desert flatlands that have sandy washes or mesquite-crowned sand hummocks which are frequently associated with rodent burrows.

They lie coiled in pits of sand or in small depressions around the shady bases of bushes during the daytime. They hibernate during the winter months, coming out as early as late February. But they are most active on warm nights during the warmer months.

Mating begins in late March and continues through May with the female giving birth to five to eighteen young in late summer or early fall. Newborn rattlers are extremely small, being only six to eight inches long.

A few misconceptions about rattlesnakes should be cleared up. One is that baby rattlers are more poisonous than their parents. Although baby rattlers are poisonous, a baby rattler's fangs are short and minute amounts of poison are not especially dangerous. Also, sidewinders do not hypnotize their prey through prolonged stares except to say that seeing one eye to eye would be enough to scare the life from anyone! And finally, for you people that believe horse hair ropes encircling the campsite will keep out sidewinders, guess again -- they will cross it as if it were not there. If left alone, the sidewinder is beneficial, eating many rodents each year.

ROADRUNNER

The roadrunner is the East Mojave's only large, ground-dwelling bird with a rather long tail. He belongs to the cuckoo family, has a large red area behind the eye, long legs, and two toes pointing forward and two pointing backwards. His tracks look like an "X" upon the ground. An older common name in some areas is the chaparral cock. He is not only found in chaparral, but deserts and pinon/juniper forests also. When startled, the shaggy crest stands up.

The roadrunner feeds on a large array of wildlife: small mammals, baby birds, bird eggs, seeds, spiders, scorpions, lizards, and snakes. He is a great lizard and snake catcher, even rattlers. He puffs up his feathers and intimidates the snake until it is exhausted, then grabs it by the back of the head, shakes it, or beats it upon the ground until dead. He swallows his food whole. He turns it length-wise so it can be easily swallowed. Occasionally a lizard tail or snake can be seen dangling from its mouth, giving the roadrunner a "cigar smoking" appearance.

April to May is the nesting season with a very crude nest being "built" in shrubs, cactus, mesquite trees, or palms from five to fifteen feet above the ground. The female lays from three to twelve white eggs in the spring; usually only four or five young hatch, or 25%. Both sexes incubate the eggs for two to three weeks with the young staying around the nest for about a month. There are many predators of young roadrunners, including coyotes, bobcats, hawks, skunks, snakes, and ravens. Sometimes, even the parents eat them.

Roadrunners are becoming more scarce as urban sprawl commences with family pets killing their share. Automobiles also take a large toll. Roadrunners are very beneficial to man, eating great quantities of insects and helping keep the reptile and rodent population in check.

KANGAROO RAT

Merriam kangaroo rats, *Dipodomys merriami,* and desert kangaroo rats, *Dipodomys deserti,* occur in the East Mojave. The kangaroo rat is one of the most common animals of the East Mojave. A distinguishing characteristic is that they live their entire lives without taking a drink of water. To make matters worse, they live in the driest regions of the world -- the desert!

TED JENSEN

The kangaroo rat is a solitary animal except during mating season. Their home range is less than a half-mile. When threatened, they use their powerful hind feet to jump straight into the air and use their long tails as a pendulum to change their direction in mid air and off they go upon landing in a different direction. They are heavily preyed upon by a wide variety of predators including kit fox, burrowing owl, rattlesnakes, coyotes, bobcats, badgers, hawks, and sometimes roadrunners. Without the kangaroo rat, the desert could be devoid of some of our most spectacular predatory animals.

The desert kangaroo rat is rather large with head and body about five to six inches long and a tail up to nine inches in length. They live up to about six years. Their habitat is fine sandy areas with sparse vegetation, usually the low desert areas. The Merriam kangaroo rat, on the other hand, is the smallest of the kangaroo rats and lives in the rocky, sandy soil also in the low desert. Merriam has a head and body about four inches and a tail five to seven inches long.

These rodents are out only during the comparatively cool hours of the night; peaks of activity run from 9 p.m. to 4 a.m. In that way, they avoid the heat stress of the intense sun. They have no sweat glands to give off valuable water to the atmosphere and they lose little water through nose and mouth.

The urine of the kangaroo rat is extremely concentrated because of their extremely efficient and powerful kidneys. This concentration requires a much smaller percentage of water to be used for expelling nitrogenous wastes (urea) from the blood. The kidneys of the kangaroo rat are about four times more efficient than man's kidneys. Also the fecal matter of the kangaroo rat has a low water content, with the utilization of the feed very high so that the amount of feces for a given amount of food is low.

Their requirement for water is very low and is met by metabolic water. Free water is formed through breaking down food, dry seeds, and plant material. By a simple chemical procedure, water is formed within the body as the nutrients are broken down to produce usable proteins for growth, repair, and reproduction.

The females give birth to one or two litters a year of one to four young in the spring and fall.

You know a kangaroo rat condominium has been found when you start to walk and the ground suddenly gives way beneath you. The ceilings of numerous burrows cave in, and you walk around like a drunk man after an earthquake. In these low desert areas in the dunes where digging is easiest, almost every strongly rooted plant has its kangaroo rat holes with well beaten paths leading in all directions to the feeding grounds. If there has been no wind, there will be many visible records of movements of these rodents as they scampered around during the night.

Kangaroo rats are both comical and docile. They are harmless to man or his crops. They do make good pets, I am told, but are better off in their wild and hostile environment.

GIANT DESERT HAIRY SCORPION

There are more than 30 species of scorpions in the United States with the largest numbers occurring in the Southwest. The desert hairy, the largest found in the U.S., has a yellow abdomen, legs, and pincers with a black "tail" rimmed in yellow. They are basically nocturnal animals coming out of their burrow shortly after the sun goes down to begin looking for food. Food consists of small animals, spiders, or insects which are stung before being devoured. Their prey is grasped in the pincers before being stung. These pincers are actually one of their mouth parts called pedipalps. Scorpions are found under logs, stones, bark, boards, and in other dark places. They show up brilliantly at night using an ultraviolet light.

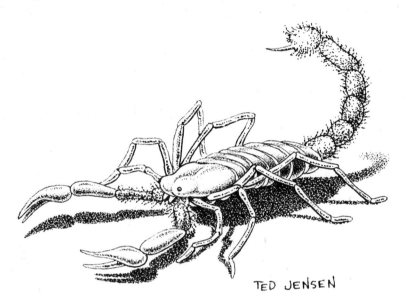

TED JENSEN

The sting of a scorpion is painful, but usually not dangerous. The poison is a neurotoxin found in two venom glands inside the tail's stinger. In Arizona there is a species of scorpion which does possess a very potent poison and can cause death in small children or unhealthy adults. As far as I know, the species does not occur in California. It is best to leave all scorpions alone unless you are positive of the species.

The female of the desert hairy scorpion produces about 30 to 40 young, born alive, which live, in their early stages of life, on their mother's back. They soon leave the mother and fend for themselves after the first week, or after the first molt, for the maternal instinct disappears early, and they could be eaten by their own mother. Quite frequently even the male is eaten by the female after mating.

Scorpions are very abundant with new species being discovered every year. They are beneficial because they feed upon insect pests.

RED-TAILED HAWK

The red-tailed hawk is our second largest hawk on the East Mojave; the largest being the ferruginous hawk. Although not abundant, they are seldom overlooked -- who can miss a large, soaring bird with a five-foot wingspan or a two-foot tall bird sitting on a telephone pole, Joshua tree, power line tower, or large rock! Many times we have seen them as we drive along the trails of the East Mojave. The birds are looking for jackrabbits or rodents the vehicles have scared up.

The red-tailed hawk builds its nest on a vertical escarpment usually over 60 feet off the ground and totally inaccessible to any non-flying animal. Sticks that are 10 to 18 inches long are the main ingredient used to build the nest which are often used year after year; mainly because the birds mate for life. From two to four eggs are laid which hatch in about 28 to 35 days with the female doing the incubating. The young have a voracious appetite which causes the mother to spend most of the day away from the nest looking for lizards, snakes, rodents, and other ground-dwelling prey. Water is obtained in their food. They will live to be about 14 years old. Never spend much time in the vicinity of a nest containing eggs or young.

The red-tailed hawk is a great benefit to ranchers due to their rodent eating habits. Populations have dwindled as a result of foolish shootings, pesticides, and destruction of their habitat.

BURROWING OWL

The burrowing owl is our only ground dwelling owl. It takes over abandoned holes of ground squirrels, badgers, or tortoises in response to a lack of cover. While other ground dwelling birds use their beaks and feet for digging burrows, the burrowing owl enlarges its burrows using only the feet.

The burrowing owl has a wingspan of about 25 inches and it is 9 to 11 inches tall. It is out during the daytime and at night. It is frequently seen outside the entrance to its burrow or on posts along the roadside. It prefers the open terrain where it can get an unobstructed view of its territory. Such a vantage point enables it to easily spot prey of insects, rodents, snakes, or lizards. It is found throughout the Southwest.

During the winter you may notice that the owl has disappeared. This is because it prefers warmer temperatures where insects and small mammals are more readily available. It does not hibernate, though. Instead it either goes to a lower altitude or latitude. It needs a food source for the winter months.

This small owl has no ear tufts, has long legs, sandy coloration, round head, and a brown back with a light, mottled breast and a short, stubby tail. It stands upright. When agitated, it bobs and bows and just before taking off, it usually bows its head. The burrowing owl also flies with an undulating up and down pattern. It can also hover when hunting insects. Sometimes when the female adults and young are severely distressed, they will give a rasping-like call that closely resembles the rattle of a rattlesnake. This may serve to warn off predators.

The nest, in the underground burrow, is located about six feet from the entrance and may be made with bits of fur, vegetation, or chips of horse or cow manure. The breeding season occurs in April or May with the young being fully grown by July. Usually six to ten white eggs are layed, a little more than an inch in length and about an inch in diameter. Since the eggs are unseen in the dark burrow, there is no need for them to be camouflaged. Both parents share the task of incubating the eggs which take about 21 days to hatch. There is only one brood of young per year.

Burrowing owls are highly beneficial to man since their staple food consists of grasshoppers and other insects. Occasionally a small rodent, mouse, lizard, or snake will also be eaten.

TARANTULA

One of the most fearsome looking creatures of the East Mojave is actually mostly harmless -- the tarantula. These spiders, arachnids, are large with sizes varying from one to five inches in length. They make burrows into the ground approximately one inch in diameter with webbing along the walls. Contrary to popular belief, they do not jump.

The time for maturity of a female tarantula is about 10 to 12 years, and she may live up to another 12 years or longer. The males are often short-lived. Tarantulas seldom bite if handled carefully. Gentle handling has never, as far as I know, led anybody to being bitten, and no deaths have ever been recorded.

The bite of the species of tarantula found in the United States is not poisonous, with a small welt appearing at the site of the bite, and no more painful than that of a bee sting. The fangs are long, though, up to one-fourth inch in a mature adult. The venom is excreted through an opening in the tip of the fang and forced into the puncture by muscular contractions around the poison glands. This is usually used for securing food.

When seeking food, this spider is not so docile. It can bite with astonishing speed. Insects make up most of its food, but also centipedes, small reptiles, and scorpions have been documented.

Most of the tarantulas seen slowly wandering about in the daytime are males looking for a mate. Following mating the female will store the male's semen in the seminal receptacles until egg laying. All spiderlings resemble the female at first, but after the last molt, the male emerges with distinctive pedipalps. The male also has claspers which he uses for grasping the female during mating.

In spite of their frightening appearance, tarantulas are harmless creatures and should never be killed. These animals aid in keeping harmful insects from becoming over-abundant.

COMMON RAVEN

Certainly it is true that, since the days of the Ice Age, birds have figured prominently in man's magic, religion, superstition, folklore, and art. In the folklore of many nations, as well as in the writings of Shakespeare, the common raven is frequently associated with ominous events or death. In an Irish tract dated around 1100 A.D., 28 different forecasts could be deduced from the behavior of ravens; each of nine different calls had a different significance.

Ravens reside in a great variety of habitats including deserts, mountains, canyons, forests, and beaches. Food preferences also have great diversity. The raven will eat almost anything including rotten fish and flesh, eggs, young birds, rats, mice and other small rodents, frogs, snails, fruits, seeds, and human garbage. Man's influence and presence in the East Mojave has helped, fortunately or unfortunately, increase the raven population. You see ravens at dumps, campsites, and along highways. Unfortunately, ravens have been blamed for severely decreasing the desert tortoise populations by eating baby tortoises. The desert tortoise is a candidate for endangered species lists.

Ravens are most often seen in pairs except when young are with their parents. There are now crows in our desert! The raven is larger than the crow and has a rounded, wedge-shaped tail. If you see a raven and a crow together, just remember "raven rounded" -- referring to the raven's rounded tail. Ravens mate for life. Their nests are built of large sticks or twigs, well interlaced, and lined with softer plant and animal material. Their nests are located in cliff areas among the rocks. The female lays four to eight blue-green, brown-spotted eggs in March or April with both parents feeding the young. Some captive ravens have been known to live to 24 years.

The raven is considered a very intelligent bird and seems to apply reasoning to situations entirely new to it. Their adaptability is remarkable. This jet-black, strong -

billed bird is enjoyable to watch.

DESERT IGUANA

We are out in the East Mojave during the hottest part of the day. There seems to be nothing stirring -- everyone is safely out of the sun's intense rays. All of a sudden, like a flash, two light-colored objects flash past us. They chase one another, bob up and down, running from one creosote bush to another, and seem to be having a ball oblivious to the great heat. They run on the tips of their toes with their legs holding their body off the hot ground. We have just seen the desert iguana or sometimes called the desert crested lizard.

TED JENSEN

Desert Iguana

The adults are light-colored, long-tailed, with a black spot behind the front legs. Some grow to be as long

269.

as two feet with most length being in tail length. The belly is white. There is a row of scales down the center of the back which can be raised when threatened, giving an awesome appearance. He prefers sandy flats, dunes, and washes.

The desert iguana loves hot weather. It keeps its body temperature around 107 degrees and can let it soar to 115 degrees -- the hottest temperature ever recorded in a North American animal. It will seek the shade of a bush or burrow if it gets too hot.

Although the desert iguana will eat an occasional insect, it is a vegetarian. It feeds on the creosote bush eating the leaves, flowers, seeds, and buds. The creosote also furnishes protection, and its base makes an excellent place for a burrow. When in the burrow, it plugs it at night to keep the moisture in and the predators out.

Desert iguanas are active from March to October and hibernate in winter. In the spring their thoughts turn to love. They pair up in April and May and usually stay together until July. In June or July eight to ten eggs can be laid, with a normal clutch of five, hatching in September. When mating, the male clasps the female's neck skin in his jaws and curls his hind legs beneath hers.

These animals are harmless. People collecting them in considerable numbers for the pet trade as well as road kills have kept the population down. Predation by roadrunners, snakes, and mammals also helps. It is now protected in California. The desert iguana has its own place in the desert and, hopefully, will remain part of it for years to come.

THE OLD WOMAN METEORITE
by Steven Pencall

The Old Woman Meteorite was found in March, 1976 by David Friberg and Mike Jendruczak of Twentynine Palms while they were looking for a legendary Spanish gold mine. It was in the crevice of a wash on the west slope of the Old Woman Mountains, approximately half way between Scanlon Gulch on the north and Brown's Wash on the south. It was found about 1.5 miles uphill from the base of the mountains at an elevation of 3,200 feet. No crater or impact scars were reported, suggesting that it fell thousands of years ago. When found, the meteorite had dimensions of 38"X34"X30" and weighed 6,080 pounds. It is the largest known meteorite from California and the second largest from the United States, surpassed only by the 15.5 ton Willamette iron meteorite found in Oregon in 1902.

Mr. Friberg and his partners filed a mining claim on the site in order to secure recovery of their find. The BLM contested the claim on the grounds that meteorites are not locatable minerals under the mining laws of the United States. A court upheld the BLM's argument and the meteorite was removed from its mountain location on June 17, 1977 by U. S. Marine Corps Heavy Helicopter Squadron 363 from the U.S.M.C. Air Station at El Toro, California.

Meteorites are debris remaining from the formation of our solar system. Most of this debris -- called meteoroids -- orbits the sun in the asteroid belt between Mars and Jupiter. Collisions with asteroids and interaction with the powerful gravitational field of Jupiter can cause meteoroids to intersect Earth orbit and fall as meteorites.

Meteorites, like Moon rocks, have tremendous scientific value because they represent samples of the solar system which have not been affected by weathering in Earth's atmosphere. The accepted age of the solar system -- 4.6 billion years -- is based on measurements of the ratios of breakdown products (daughter elements) resulting from decay of radioactive elements in meteorites. By contrast, the oldest known Earth rocks, recently found in northern Canada, are slightly more than 3.9 billion years old. Therefore, meteorites and certain Moon rocks are the only record of the first 700 million years of the solar system.

The Old Woman Meteorite is an iron meteorite, which accounts for its exceptional size. It consists of iron containing about 6% nickel with lesser amounts of cobalt, phosphorus, and sulphur. The other major meteorite classes, stone or stony iron meteorites, tend to break into smaller fragments as they pass through the atmosphere.

A large portion of the Old Woman Meteorite is generally on display at the BLM Desert Information Center in Barstow, although it is loaned to other museums periodically, in which case, a replica is displayed in its place. The portion on display weighs 5,128 pounds -- the smaller portion resides in the collection of the Smithsonian Institution in Washington, D.C.

HARD ROCK MINING
by Tom Cooper

As a young man, Tom Cooper worked as a hard rock miner in the Lucky Jim Mine on the east side of the Old Woman Mountains in 1930. It is our good fortune that he prepared a lengthy manuscript describing his experiences in the Lucky Jim. The following pages contain an extract from that manuscript. I'm encouraged to reproduce it here because of the response I received after reading a part of this account over CB during the trek over the Fourth Segment EMHT this past fall. The Fourth Segment passes very close to the Lucky Jim; hopefully, a reading of Tom's account will discourage you from exploring this or any other desert mine -- they're dangerous!

I have heard there are over ten thousand prospects and mines in the desert areas of Southern California. I know that I am responsible for eight or ten of the prospects or pot-holes. The pot-holes could be anything from a trench two or three feet deep and three or four feet square, to a horizontal tunnel or vertical shaft from five to twenty-five feet in length or depth.

Just how much underground work in the way of shafts, tunnels, cross-cuts, drifts or stopes it takes to be called a mine I don't know. Some of the big mines in the United States and in the world figure the underground development work in miles. Some smaller mines figure their underground work in so many thousand feet.

The silver mine we had leased (the Lucky Jim -- Old Woman Mountains) had about 1,150 feet of development work. The main tunnel or adit was driven in from the side of a mountain, horizontally, for 750 feet. This tunnel ended at a station or room about 10 feet wide and 12 feet long.

We had to buy and install several great timbers, 10"X10"X18', with stulls and lagging. From the room, a crosscut was driven northward for 200 feet. At this point the air was getting bad and when our compressor was set up, we installed a booster tank and pump and ran an air line to the end of the crosscut both for breathing air and drilling air (for the jackhammers).

A drift ran off at the opposite side of the station, in country rock, for about 115 feet. This was an exploration tunnel, searching for additional veins or bodies of ore. At the head of this drift was a mass of bats, probably several thousand, and during the first few days of our looking over the underground workings we had some interesting experiences with bats.

We had been told there were bats in the mine, but we had no idea there were so very many. From the way the bats swarmed in and out, it would indicate they had not been disturbed by man, or anything else, for many, many years.

At the station some enterprising souls had sunk a winze (a vertical shaft within a mine) 85 feet deep. Like the ridiculously large unsupported station at the end of the 750 feet tunnel, the winze was ridiculous in size, about six feet square. This winze may have been done with a double cage arrangement to support plans for sinking to a great depth.

In addition to the already described tunnels and developments in "our" mine, there was also an abandoned and caved-in stope which was, in a short time, destined to be the cause of one of the most hair-raising experiences of my life. As time went on, we attempted to drive a raise (escape tunnel) to the surface. This work had to be abandoned just 75 feet from the surface when the equipment we had was just not of sufficient capacity to complete the job.

For a short time some hand drilling was done before the compressor, receiver tank, booster tank, pipe, pneumatic hammers or jackhammers, or rock drills, and power plant were received at the mine and set up for operation. Hand drilling in hard rock is, I might say, quite an art. A lot of the art is in staying with it even though your arms and shoulders feel about as stiff as the rock you are drilling, and at best you are in an awkward position, sitting or standing in a black tunnel, far underground, and just a small miner's carbide lamp as the only light to see what you are doing.

Coming out of the city with soft hands, soft muscles, no mining experience and my first day at hand drilling, I managed to get a hole down 17 inches. I was advised to start with a four pound single-jack (hammer). At the end of the second day my right arm went "dead" -- numb, and I could not lift my arm. It took over two days for my arm to get back to normal and when I resumed the hand drilling with a six pound hammer, I practiced, and was able to change over from right hand to left hand, with rest intervals, and I found that both arms became afflicted with that numbness that makes the arms useless. However I kept going day after day.

The callouses formed on my hands, but did not blister and in time my hands were really tough and hard, and the muscles in my arms, shoulder, and chest were getting as hard and tough as my hands. I was asked one day how many holes the three men who were drilling by

(above) Chemist at the Lucky Jim Mine standing in front of early living quarters.

(right) Thomas M. Cooper at his cabin at the Lucky Jim Mine, 1929-1930.

October 1931

both Thomas M. Cooper Collection

hand, had drilled, and how deep were the holes. I replied that we had drilled about five holes from seventeen to twenty inches deep. My answer really proved my inexperience in the type of mining we were engaged in. Hand drilling is hard, slow work, and in reporting how deep a hole is, a fraction of an inch is well worth reporting, such as seventeen and a quarter inches or seventeen and a half inches, not "seventeen to twenty inches."

Then there is the planning of the number of holes, the exact depth, the placing of the holes in the face of rock to be blown out, and the angle of each hole so that the rock will be broken and blown out according to plan. It is interesting to follow the progress of tunnel work in a mine under the direction of a good mining engineer. When the compressed air was put into use and pneumatic jackhammers (rock drills) were put into use, the holes to shoot each day, were, of course, much deeper than the hand drilled holes.

The work of mucking out the face of the tunnel of the loose rock after a round of holes had been shot is a hard job. The steel ore cars are rolled up the narrow gauge track line. In "our" mine all hands -- the president, vice-president, secretary-treasurer, and all corporate members including stock holders, were jacks-of-all-trades: blacksmiths, carpenters, drillers, muckers, powder monkeys, truck drivers, track layers, and a hundred other skilled and unskilled jobs.

It was decided in due time to explore the winze that had been sunk at the station. We understood it to be 85 feet deep. There was no collar set around the top of the winze and the loose rock made it hazardous to stand too close to the edges. We threw two 8"X8" stulls across

278.

(above) Visitors and investors from Los Angeles.
Lucky Jim Mine, March 1930
(below) Prospecting around Turtle Mtns February 1932.
both Thomas M. Cooper Collection

the winze, lowered a carbide lamp on a rope, and we verified the fact that the winze was right at 85 feet deep. The next few days were devoted to cutting trenches in the rock at all four corners of the winze so that 8'X8' timbers could be fitted in these grooves or trenches. And then a wood platform or floor laid over the winze, or the hole, with an opening 4'X4' to be used as a work opening.

I was lowered by hand down this winze in an ore bucket fastened to a rope. If this had been done down the side of an 85 feet cliff or down the side of an 85 feet building, I would have been scared to death. The fact was it was utter blackness in that winze, and my carbide lamp produced only a feeble light as I swung and descended down and down. I could not see the bottom of the winze and most of the time I could not even see the sides even though they were not more than one to three feet from me.

At the bottom of the winze I found that the men who did the work down there were very neat and tidy. There was practically no loose rock -- just those that had been dropped down in an effort to judge the depth. I did find, however, the skeleton of a snake and what appeared to be the skeletons of two rabbits. There were over ten people at the mine and there were over ten opinions as to how a snake and two rabbits would travel 750 feet along a tunnel and then fall down a hole in the ground.

It was decided that some exploration work would be done at the face of a 200 feet cross-cut. The air at the end of the cross-cut was very bad. We brought some air in, as mentioned earlier, by way of a pipeline from the air compressor 950 feet away at the surface. It became necessary to drive a raise to the surface at this point, which would be a distance of about 150 feet.

This all came to an end when the work in the raise had progressed to within 75 feet of the surface. The air was becoming too bad to breathe, and the temperature was unbearable. The deciding factor to abandon the raise was when the big stoper drill vibrated lose. I was climbing up the ladder in the raise and did not hear the stoper drill making its machine-gun noise of hammering the drill steel against the rock. But I did hear a peculiar noise. I had a large carbide lamp with a six inch reflector and as I neared the working platform I put the light on a frightening scene. The stoper is about six or seven feet long. The working space where the man was working was about three feet square. We were still able to get 100 to 120 pounds of air pressure and when the stoper broke loose, the operator had been unable to "cut the air" -- the lever to shut off the air valve.

The operator was groping around trying to grab hold on that lever and at the same time had to be very careful not to let the wiggling, twisting, writhing, 50 pound stoper strike him or mash him against the rock on all sides. The next few seconds were packed with all the excitement I wanted for some time.

I could not get up on the working platform to help my co-worker because of the thrashing, twisting stoper. All I could do was just stand on the rung on the ladder and give a word of encouragement. At one time when the stoper came to a position where I thought I might grab the shut-off lever, my grab was short and the stoper took a new twist and was gone. The driller finally made a lunge at the stoper, got the shut-off valve closed, and the wild scene was over.

The wild scene was over to be sure, but it left a nasty injury to the driller. His left hand seemed to be

281.

badly mashed. It must have been a painful ordeal, going down the ladder, and hunching along nearly a thousand feet of tunnel with that hand torn and bleeding. My friend was taken to Needles where he obtained medical aid. Along with numerous abrasions and cuts, one finger was broken.

There were long stretches of tunnel that had no lagging timbers, or no timbering at all. One day two or three of the more experienced mining engineers in our party were giving both the foot wall and the hanging wall of one of the tunnels a close inspection. When I joined these men they pointed out rock formations that, to me, looked like huge blisters or bulges. I was told they were known as "kidneys" or "sticks" or "slickensides." The tunnel where the "kidneys" occurred was a big one and the slabs were big. The next day we were looking this spot over again when one of the "kidneys" slipped and flopped over on the tunnel floor. We estimated the chunk of rock to weigh about three tons. The uncanny thing about it was the fact that the three ton slab of rock slithered off the wall of the tunnel with amazingly little noise. Several times we saw these "slickensides" slip from the wall to the floor of the tunnel.

One day when I was walking along the "danger zone" I was trying to be careful. I had the big carbide lamp with the six inch reflector, and was watching both sides, when the very thing we had been talking about happened. A large kidney or slab of slick rock silently slithered lose just as I was passing it. It took probably one or two seconds to see the movement and I guess the reflexes must have come into action at the split second the brain impulse occurred.

I made a backward leap that was later measured at

(above) The road to Milligan on Santa Fe R.R.
October 1931
(below) The platform at Milligan where ore was shipped.
both Thomas M. Cooper Collection

over six feet and I must have been in a hunched position due to the fact that I did not strike my head on the roof of the tunnel. That slab of rock was estimated to be over five tons and I am glad that I was able to make such a good backward leap. None of us liked the job of breaking these slabs of rock up and then loading in ore cars to be run out and dumped down the mine dump. It was all hard, backbreaking work with no return as it was not a profitable ore.

The next time I came upon the engineers was in a section of tunnel that was heavily timbered, namely the main, 750 feet tunnel. Most of the timbers used were 6"X6" and 8"X8". Upon examining the 6"X6" timbers that were laid between the roof of the tunnel and the upright support timbers, we found some of the 6"X6"s had been compressed and squeezed down to a thickness of just one inch at a point where it rested on the supporting timber.

The engineers pointed out that timbers compressed by the pressure of the rock above it to a one inch thickness had lost all its strength and that particular portion of the tunnel roof was actually not supported at all. A geologist would have his geological bonanza in that tunnel. The entire length -- 750 feet -- was a continuous series of fractures, faults, and every exception to the rule. The earthquakes, tremors, and I guess volcanoes, and other earth crust movements, must have been unusually severe in this region. The cost of replacing those timbers, to say nothing of the extreme hazard, was out of the question for us. In the meantime it was not helpful, going in and out of that tunnel two or four times a day, knowing that many of the supporting timbers were useless.

There was never a dull day during this mining

venture. Two or three wives braved the vigors of the desert and came out for a visit to our mine in this really remote region. While the wives were there I learned some of the superstitions. The first superstition was that it is very taboo for a woman to enter a mine. Never take a dog or cat or any domestic animal in a mine. Never whistle or sing inside a mine, and many others. It was never explained, even by the old-timers, just what significance there is to any of the superstitions, or where and how they got started. One of our group, who was born in England, and was at one time connected with the tin mining industry in England, was referred to at times as a "cousin jack." It was explained to me that English miners, or at least some of them, are sometimes known as cousin jacks.

The men and the mining engineers who were responsible for driving the main tunnel 750 feet into the side of the mountain where the mine was located are to be commended for a clever job well done. This tunnel was driven many years ago, probably around 1911. The outstanding achievement was the grade maintained for the 750 feet. The grade was so gentle that heavy, steel ore cars with heavy solid steel wheels, about eight inches in diameter and the car itself measuring about 24 inches wide, 30 inches deep, and 48 inches long, would roll right along. In other words, the ore cars were heavy contraptions themselves even when empty. But it took no great effort to push one of the cars the entire length of the tunnel.

When the ore car was loaded with rock or ore, it weighed well over a ton and the almost perfect grading of the tunnel made it possible for one man to push the car to the surface with such ease that at times there would be stretches of 50 to 150 feet where the ore car would start to roll free and pick up momentum.

At first I would try to hold the car back, but soon I learned to "let'r rip." I'd jump on the back, hang on, and really get a ride that could not be equalled in any amusement park. There was one section about half way along the tunnel where the grading was just right for the ore cars to "take off" on their own. Lady luck was with me on one of those tunnel trips. Unknown to me the ore car had not been properly loaded. It was heavy at the rear end. I hit the magic stretch where I had experienced the wild, free rides. We, the ore car, the load of rock, and myself, were barrelling along at a good clip when suddenly a piece of rock on the small, narrow gage track, or a loose section in one of the rails, caused the improperly loaded ore car to tip up at the heavy end, which was the end where I was riding.

It all happened in seconds. Fortunately the heavy ore car tipped up, then rolled over on one side. I was badly dazed, and possibly, might have been knocked out for a few seconds. I had a bad lump for several days on the right cheek bone. It might have been a more grim story if I had slipped under the ore car. The same thing happened to one of our other men who did not learn a lesson from my experience.

I had the job of cleaning the rock out of the tunnel, cleaning up the mess, and then getting the narrow gage track back in operation. I will admit I "rode" the ore cars many times after my accident. But just a few feet at a time and standing on a steel plate fastened to the rear end and I was able to jump if need be and let the ore go.

Our mine was located midway up a box canyon that was two miles from the open valley to the closed end

The "boys" at the Lucky Jim Mine decided
to collect honey from a bee hive in a rock cliff near
Sunflower Springs. They didn't get much honey. Their
protective "costumes" prompted this "bull fight."
There wasn't much in the way of entertainment
at the Lucky Jim in March of 1930!

Thomas M. Cooper Collection

of the canyon which was a steep slope up a mountain. The wind would roar down that canyon with the most amazing force for such a short distance traveled. All our cabins were reinforced with heavy 6"X6" timbers used as props on the down side.

A fire started one night when the canyon wind was exceptionally wild. About 11 p.m. one of our mining engineers was pumping air into the gasoline tank of a Coleman lantern. The big mistake was that the air was pumped into the tank while the lantern was lighted. Suddenly the pump plunger pulled out and gasoline, under pressure, sprayed out, became ignited, and in seconds the whole cabin was in flames. Ordinarily our camp, due to the fact that we were usually up and going long before sunup, was always dark and all hands sound asleep before 10 p.m. Due to the terrific wind that night I was out of bed at 11 p.m. to make sure that my cabin was not going to take off down the canyon in the high wind. I looked out a window and saw a red glow in the window of the large cabin where we cooked and had our meals. One of the engineers lived in that cabin.

In split seconds I had boots on and was out of my cabin yelling my head off to arouse the rest of the camp. The interior of the cabin was in a chaotic mess. Gasoline had spilled on the long dining table and was burning with an unusual lot of smoke. Most of our food supplies were in the cook shack attached to one end of the cabin. But that section seemed relatively safe for the time being at least. Somehow the windows in this cabin had been fitted with a kitchen type of curtain and one of these curtains was burning fiercely as gasoline must have spattered on it.

There was not enough water in the camp to even consider using it. It was disheartening to think of losing that main cabin which housed our cooking facility, our homemade desert cooler, our food supply, and eating quarters, as well as living quarters for one of our most experienced mining engineers and geologists, with his library of most interesting technical books. All these thoughts raced through the minds of all of us in quick seconds and soon all hands had blankets and large ore sacks. One man, wearing heavy, corduroy pants, ripped them off and had that window curtain fire out in no time.

The rest of us battered the flames on the table, on the floor, and on a section of the wall. The smoke was bad, but it was all over quickly and we were a really grateful crew to know that we had not been burned out. We did have one casualty however. The left hand of the mining engineer was burned and one or two nasty blisters formed. The hand was treated and loosely dressed. It took many days before it was normal. The next morning all our gasoline lanterns were inspected and repairs and adjustments made.

Another frustrating experience, on the comical side, gave all hands at the mine a good laugh. We were always in need of lumber. Our immediate requirements, however, were for timbers up to 12"X12" and heavy 2"X12" and 3"X12" lagging. There was on a hillside, near the blacksmith shop, a pile of forty or fifty 2"X4"s, 16 feet long. We finally had need of 2X4s and I volunteered to cut or saw the supply we had on hand.

I started on the first 2X4 in all seriousness, and sawed and sawed and noticed I was not making any kind of a cut in the 2X4 which should have been cut through long ago. I thought maybe I might have been trying to cut through a hard knot, but after having a good look, there was no knot. What I did not notice was that half a dozen men had gathered in the blacksmith shop to watch the "tenderfoot" saw, or try to saw, the desert hardened 2X4s.

I really worked on the 2X4 and all my seriousness and hard work were giving my hidden audience a great laugh as they knew the lumber that was giving me such a hard time had been exposed to the desert elements too long and was in almost a rock hard condition, but not as brittle as rock. As time went on I became curious about the hardness of the 2X4 pieces of wood.

I put one of the 2X4s over two rocks and tried to break it with a 16 pound sledge hammer. The first blow was, I thought, a good healthy swing at the 2X4. But nothing happened. The next blow at the 2X4, I slammed the 16 pound hammer down as hard as I could. The hammer was bounced up over my head and went sailing out in the wild blue yonder. The 2X4 did not have a noticeable dent in it and the hammer was found 30 feet away. I was lucky the hammer did not hit me. And as far as I am concerned that pile of 2X4s is still out there on the hillside in the desert getting harder and harder.

DESERT LITERATURE

To this point, we have not said much about the literature of the desert. Here and there reference has been made to other books that the traveler might consult for more details about the cultural or natural history of the desert -- but the subject of the literature itself has not been addressed.

That wasn't an inadvertent oversight. We've simply been waiting for the right time and for the space in one of the guides.

Interesting enough, the literature of the desert, from the voices of those who have experienced it firsthand, turns out to be the most enduring treasure of the desert. The literature itself is the only aspect of the desert that will remain unchanged. Take this book, for example, you can assume that 100 years from now a copy of it can be located and it will say exactly the same things it says now. Perhaps no other aspect of the desert will be the same 100 years from now as it is today.

The body of literature dealing with the Mojave Desert is relatively modest, but it is growing rapidly just now. In the past 10 years, as we have been struggling with problems of how to manage the desert into the future, literally hundreds of studies covering every aspect have appeared. These are in some cases labors for pay and not always labors of love and this is reflected in the quality and thoroughness of the work. Still, it has focused attention on the rich cultural and natural history of the desert and it has inspired a number of capable individuals to work in the field.

Material of useful and lasting value about the desert generally appears only after the author has

ELZA IVAN EDWARDS
1897-1984
Dean of the desert writers,
"Eddie," as his friends called him,
was also an eloquent speaker. He challenged
desert enthusiast to write about their desert, but
"Remember, it is not enough to wear out the seat of
your pants in a library, you must also
wear out a pair of boots!"

This picture was taken in 1964
at the Author's Breakfast at the annual
Death Valley Encampment.

292.

thoroughly researched his subject and has gained the necessary understanding and "feel" of the desert. Hence we have the immense value of David G. Thompson's *Mohave Desert Region* published in 1929. By that time, Thompson, an employee of the U.S.G.S., had more than ten years of association with the Mojave Desert. His interest had gone far beyond the bureaucratic requirements of his position with the Geological Survey.

The desert will be a much richer place if you can review some of the literature. It is one thing, for example, to know the basic history of the old Salt Lake Trail -- that it was a wagon road connecting Los Angeles with Salt Lake City beginning in 1849; that for many years Mormon freight trains plied over that trail between Utah and the seaport at San Pedro for goods that they couldn't grow and manufacture in Utah; that the United States Mails were carried over this route; that this route is the forerunner of the present Interstate 15. It is quite another thing to read firsthand accounts of the men and women who used the trail -- to read the words they chose to describe their reactions to the desert and their sufferings on the long stretches without water.

It has been the objective from the beginning to bring that firsthand flavor into the guide books. We do that by quoting from original sources as much as possible. When we do that we try to quote sources previously not published or at least not readily available. There is a real limit of how much of that we can do. It is our hope that you'll become interested in reading more and that you'll pursue that interest into the general body of desert literature. That's what this section is about. How do you go about that?

When I first became seriously interested in the

literature of the desert, back in about 1960, it was my great fortune to have stumbled into a good library and to have discovered the wonderful desert bibliography written by E. I. Edwards. Subsequently, "Eddie," as he was known by his friends ("Eddie" is deceased now) became my friend and mentor and I now own his desert library.

Actually, Eddie wrote three desert bibliographies. In fact, I'll confess to having laid a trap, I used the words "treasure," "voices," and "enduring" all in the same sentence. This is because Eddie's bibliographies were named *Desert Treasure* (1948), *Desert Voices* (1958), and *The Enduring Desert* (1969).

Eddie was one of those persons who cared very much about words. He used the word "treasure" because, to him, the literature of the desert was one of its greatest treasures. He used the word "voices" because he saw the literature of the desert being the true voice of the desert. He used the word "enduring" because, by that late point in his life, he recognized that the desert that he knew and loved would endure only in the literature.

All the literature of the desert, known to Eddie, was listed in *The Enduring Desert*. He wrote descriptive bibliographies -- that is, he not only listed the books, he described and evaluated them. His book was so useful (even at that early period) that the reference librarians had gone through it and written down the call numbers of those books in his bibliography that existed in their holdings.

The Enduring Desert is a fairly rare book, but most good libraries will have recognized its value and procured a copy when it was issued. Today, on the rare book market, a good copy of this book can cost up to about $100.00.

The Enduring Desert will introduce you to the literature of the desert, and it will also introduce you to the man E. I. Edwards -- both are rewarding experiences. Once you begin delving into the published literature (and mainly that's what is in Eddie's bibliographies, published literature) you'll find that many of the books make reference to other books, perhaps books not listed in the bibliography.

If you are interested enough, you can commence building a collection of your favorites. This, too, is a rewarding experience. You can review them over and over again. Many will be expensive, but good desert books have proven to be investments that hold their value and many appreciate.

Unfortunately, Eddie's bibliography ends in 1969 and there is no update. Much has appeared since then, in book form, in periodicals, and from government agencies. There is no road map. You'll have to pursue the subject in the libraries and with Western Americana book dealers. We make reference to some of the broader-scope and more comprehensive works in the guides.

In addition to the published literature, there is that whole body of information referred to as "source" material or unpublished manuscript materials. This is the stuff that the great books about the desert will be based upon. I'm referring to early newspapers, diaries and journals from the early days, reminiscences from people who have been on the desert a long time, old letters, and photos. A person conscious of and appreciative of the need to understand the history of the desert, watches constantly for these things.

Frequently, source materials are vulnerable in the sense that they may perish. For example, in connection with preparing material for this series of Guides, we interviewed a person who had firsthand knowledge of the boom camp of Greenwater, near Death Valley. She had prepared a written account of her recollections -- that much of what she knows is not perishable so long as a copy of that written material is protected. Then there was the opportunity to interview her on tape (oral history) to gain more. In this case, material and insights that might otherwise have been lost are saved. Our understanding of places and events becomes richer.

I mention this here to enlist your support in finding obscure material pertaining to the desert and to solicit your help in saving it. You can help by contacting the *Friends,* or you can obtain copies of photos and material for local historical societies and educational groups.

In closing this discussion about the literature of the desert, we'll quote from *The Enduring Desert* itself and let Eddie explain it to you his way. Listen to his words carefully, and recognize that one of the most enduring and rewarding treasures of the desert is its literature. Go seek it and you will be enriched.

"*The Enduring Desert*, therefore, is a new and enriched documentary treatise of California desert literature. The book is essentially a directional guide to the superb narrative of our desert country -- its flowers and shrubs and trees and cacti, its birds and animals, its canyons and mountains and valleys, its old ghost-town mining camps, its sunrises and sunsets, its penetrant silences. It is an index to the history, drama, philosophy, and adventure which are all inextricably woven into the pattern of our desert fabric by hundreds of devoted writers -- many of them prominent, others not so well known; but each, to the extent of his or her ability, depicting some brilliantly conceived facet of the desert's romantic story.

"Over the long years of close, personal contact with the desert, both as its guest and its resident, I have visited and explored many of the areas described in the books listed in this volume. In common with other desert lovers I have witnessed ancient landmarks vanish from the land. Much of the desert I once knew and loved has been submerged by the inexorable encroachment of the thing we loosely refer to as 'civilization.' Desert plants and animals are retreating before the inevitable deluge of homes and towns and industries, else they are being crushed by its unrelenting pressure.

"Happily, the quiet, restful land that is so rapidly losing its physical character shall remain enshrined in the writings of these dedicated men and women whose creative interpretations are recorded in this book. Because of them the land and its memories shall forever live vibrantly within our minds and hearts -- a viable, *enduring* desert."

INDEX

298.

301.

UNITED STATES GEOLOGICAL SURVEY MAPS

The U.S.G.S. produces a great variety of topographical maps for every state in the United States. They provide great detail and consequently can add much to a backcountry experience. Also, good maps can be an indispensable survival tool if things go wrong. There are maps covering the East Mojave in both the 15 minute and 7.5 minute series. The 15 minute maps tend to be 30 years old or older. Still they show much useful information. The 7.5 minute series is based upon much more recent data.

LIST OF TOPOGRAPHICAL MAPS
HERITAGE TRAIL -- FENNER TO NEEDLES

15 MINUTE
Bannock
Essex
Milligan
Needles
Savahia Peak
Sawtooth Range
Stepladder Mountains
Turtle Mountains
Whipple Mountains

7.5 MINUTE
Castle Rock
Chemehuevi Peak
Essex
Fenner
Fenner Spring
Falttop Mountain
Havasu Lake
Little Piute Mountains

7.5 MINUTE (cont.)
Mohawk Spring
Monumental Pass
Mopah Peaks
Needles
Needles SW
Old Woman Statue
Painted Rock Wash
Savahia Peak
Savahia Peak NE
Savahia Peak NW
Savahia Peak SW
Snaggletooth
Stepladder Mountain NE
Topock
W of Juniper Mine
W of Mohawk Spring
Whale Mountain
Whipple Mts. SW
Wilhelm Spring

A complete selection of U.S.G.S. maps
is available over the counter at:

Allied Services
966 North Main Street
Orange, California 92667
714-637-8824

TED JENSEN

Neal Johns is the principal "pathfinder" for the East Mojave Heritage Trail. He has had responsibility for development of the road logs. He has done more field work on the Trail than anyone and he has coordinated the efforts of the *Friends* who check the log out prior to publication. He also reviews the development manuscripts prior to publication.

TED JENSEN

As with the three previous EMHT Guides, Bob Martin has continued in the role of Chief Cartographer for the *Friends*. All the maps in the book were created by him. Bob has worked hand in hand with Neal Johns to make the changes to the road log and maps as they become perfected. A great share of the effectiveness of our Guides is attributable to Bob's wonderful maps. Additionally, Bob and Marilyn Martin have done much field work and they provide us with a valuable review of the manuscripts prior to publication.